IDENTITY THEFT:

Who's Behind the Mask?

Discover significance and
freedom in finding who
you are

By Sandi King Kramer

ISBN: 1-59684-217-2
©Copyright 2006 by
Sandi Kramer Ministries
Printed by Derek Press
Cleveland, TN

Table of Contents

Dedication

This book is dedicated to my faithful, loving husband Rick, who gives me the wings to fly and inspires me to pursue my dreams. Thank you for putting up with all my "silly" ideas, sleepless nights, and hilarious incidents. Thanks for all the years of laughter, for the life you've given back to me and loving memories. I love spending my life with you.

To my daddy, R. Edwin King, who loved me unconditionally and showed me the love of what a father should be. He was my Jesus with skin on.

To my mother, and my friend, Sylvia Case King, thank you for praying me through all my days. I am so grateful and thankful to God for picking you out for me, to be my mother.

To my sister, Gail, who I admire and appreciate so much for all she has taught me through the years.

To my children, Ryan, Lacey, Brandon, and King, thank you for teaching me how to be a mother and being patient with me. I learn so much from each one of you individually. You are all such a wonderful gift from God to me. I am honored and privileged to be called, your mom.

And to the writers of this book, thank you for your honesty and openness in allowing people to know the "real" you, I applaud you. May the Lord openly reward you as you have abundantly blessed my life.

Foreword

During the summer of 1986, I began to feel very strongly that the Lord was calling me into full time ministry. This calling was very clear. However, my struggle to respond was very cloudy. I could not imagine how God could use someone like me in ministry. I had no family in ministry... I was completely inexperienced...my knowledge of the Word was at best sub-par...my prayer life stunk...I didn't have what I thought it took. But I could not get away from that clear voice of God..."if you will only say yes and be obedient, I will surround you with individuals to assist you in fulfilling this calling." Thank God that He knows the plans He has for us...to prosper, not to harm us, to give us a hope and a future.

I could not have even begun to imagine all of the incredible people who would come into my life over these twenty years of ministry to students. One of the greatest ladies I have had the honor to work with is Sandi Kramer. She is indeed a partner in ministry and a true sister in the Lord. Several years ago, Sandi and I served together at the North Cleveland Church of God. I was the youth pastor and Sandi worked as a teacher to our young ladies. I remember the day Sandi sat in my office and shared her passion for young ladies, while tears ran down her face. I began to see God birth in her a sincerity to make a difference in the lives of young women in our area. I also know that God had a plan to use her passion and her story in a bigger way. Now that I have had the opportunity to read her story on paper, I am even more convinced of God's call on her life.

This generation needs to hear her honesty as well as those others who have contributed their own personal story. This book, Identity Theft – Who's Behind the Mask, has truly come from a heart for what God wants to do in the lives of young people. Sandi believes in young people and their potential. She is willing to do more than just sit back and let things remain the same. She is making a difference This book is a testimony to that fact. I thank God for Sandi and the other contributors for their dedication to the call of God on their lives. What a hope…what a future!

Kevin Kelley
Student Ministries Pastor

Introduction

The book, "Identity Theft – Who's Behind the Mask?" is for every one of all ages. The Bible says our adversary Satan is out to steal, kill, and destroy. It matters not what age you are, race or gender. He tries to rob us; God's cherished people, of our own identity in Christ.

We will search in someone else or some thing that is incapable of fulfilling the emptiness we feel in our heart. The emptiness felt comes from the lack of positive relationships, the missing parent or perhaps the abuse that took place in our life.

For myself, my identity was wrapped in whatever my older sister said I liked or did not like. I have come to understand that in the birth order, I am not alone.

Talking with people everywhere I go, I get the same response from the "babies" of the family. We search to find identity in a boyfriend, a husband, a sister, a friend or occupation.

It is an unrealistic expectation to think a person who is fallible or a career that is a sense of false security can fulfill our desires and will meet our every need, emotionally, physically, mentally and spiritually.

For some of us we know who our parents are in Christ; our Pastor is in Christ, but we find ourselves lost striving to find our own identity. The challenge is we don't know who we are in Christ. All I knew was that I was Ed and Sylvia's baby and Gail's sister.

So many people of influence in our lives breathe on us their perception of what we should do, how we should act, what we should look like, what makes us fulfilled, what our career should be. That is not all bad, if they are a positive influence in our lives. But we rely more on their opinion rather than asking Father what His purpose is for our lives. When in reality, we should research the Word to read what He says we are to be.

As humanity longs for approval, attention, someone to love unconditionally, the only place we will find a perfect love, a perfect relationship is in Christ Jesus. The longing within our soul to please others causes us to lose our identity, drowning in their perception of who we are.

Everyone at some point in their life asks themselves the question – Who Am I Really? What do I really like? What really makes me happy? In this book, you will read my story of how I found my identity in Christ and the journey I went through along with five wonderful, triumphant young people and their personal journeys and experiences.

This is an incredible book to read. You don't have to wait until you are older in age to know you can find your identity in Jesus Christ our Savior. He waits. He longs for you. He leaps for joy thinking about you. He is crazy about you. When you speak His name, He smiles. He's passionate about you. He fights for you. He died for you. He rose for you. Soon the lover of your soul is coming back for you!

Our prayer for you as you read this book is for you to hunger to know Him and to find your identity in what He says about you. It is time to take the mask off and to be real with your Maker. We pray that you will find a greater passion for

His approval than man's approval. Man may stand and applaud you but the applause will surely grow faint.

Your heavenly Father applauds you cheering you on as you walk through your journey in this life. The stories In this book will amaze you.

Do I like Peas?

There was a little girl, who had a disease to please,
She would even ask her older sister, "Do I like peas?"

Her identity was wrapped up in the opinion of others,
What anyone said she was, she would wear on her
shoulders.

A chameleon she would be in the midst of the crowd,
Please, please can I just make somebody proud?

I just wanted to be accepted, "Do you really like me?"
I don't know who I am; will you please tell me who I'll be?

In a still quiet voice her heavenly Father would say,
"You're my sweet girlie girl, please trust and obey.

You are my Modern Day Esther, the one I love,
You are forever accepted from your King above.

I've held you and nurtured you through your faceless years,
There's always been a place in my heart you have held so
dear.

I gave you my Son; my Spirit dwells within you,
You are my chosen vessel, I chose to work through."

My identity no longer is in the approval of man,
Jesus is my solid rock, with Him I can stand.

Nestled in the arms of my Father above,
I'm safe and secure, accepted by my Beloved.

Sandi King Kramer

Chapter One
A Disease to Please

My sister was four years older than I. She always did what was right. She made great decisions, and whatever decision she made she followed through with it and was a success, unlike myself. When we were younger I would always ask her what I liked no matter what it was. I remember on one occasion we were at my grandparents' house in California and my grandmother asked me, "Would I like some peas?" I recall sitting at the dinner table looking over to my older sister asking her, "Gail, do I like peas?" She said, "No, shaking her head you don't like peas." I will tell you, it may have taken me a long time to know this but I do like snappy sugar peas.

I had an incredible family. My daddy was a minister so I was known as a PK, a preacher's kid. I always felt being a preacher's kid was an honor; however, we had to live up to standards that were imposed by man. Our family was much like the television show "Leave it to Beaver." My sister was Wally and I was the Beave. I can hear myself now like the Beave, saying, "Gosh, Gail, why do we do that?" Mom always had dinner on the table and Father always knew best. Yes, I was blessed. I cherish my childhood days. Because of my father's occupation we got to travel the world. We lived in South Carolina, California, Texas, Europe and Tennessee. One Easter break, Daddy took us to 21 different countries. It was in Europe when I remember my sister telling me that she was going off to college. She was going to leave me over in a foreign country without my identity, my sister. I was devastated. We were so close.

When either one of us were in the shower the other one would come and sit on the commode just to talk so neither one of us would be alone.

After I survived the year without my sister's identity, at a critical age of 15, over weight, no self-esteem and no concept of who I was, I found myself desiring the approval of one young man. He was also a preacher's kid and we both lived up to the old saying, "the worst ones are the preacher's kids or the deacon's kids." At the age of 16, I chose to give him myself, my virginity. I was always an honest child so I confessed to my father and mother at what our denomination calls, the general assembly. This general assembly was held in Texas and I couldn't keep my private pain to myself any longer. We were such a close-knit family. At these assemblies they have long meetings during the day discussing church policy and during the evenings they had church. After church one late night, I announced to my daddy and mother (whom I loved so much and they loved me) that their baby girl was no longer a virgin. I knew my timing was bad, but I had to confess. I was always taught true confession was good for the soul. Boy, did I ever wear that motto out through the years. It seemed like every time I turned around I was confessing something. I knew I had disappointed them so badly. I thought my heart was going to jump right out of my chest cavity.

After Daddy served his term in California, we moved to the small city of Cleveland, Tennessee. I call it CleVegas. What happens in CleVegas stays in CleVegas. Whatever you wanted there you could get it. I went to a Christian college. I was a cheerleader for a semester and thought life was grand, all along still searching for my own identity. I

2

always lived under mom and dad's rules. Whether I obeyed them or not was a different story. My parents had an incredible relationship with Christ, not a religion. I personally knew of Jesus Christ, but I didn't know how to live with Him. My daddy was my God. He always had the right answer; he was my financial provider, whatever I needed I went to him and he supplied it. At the time, I was still living at home, going to college, and living each day to its fullest, having sex with my boyfriend, the preacher's kid. We dated other people between times but somehow we always ended up together. A year before we came to Cleveland, he decided to attend the same college. We both lived in Europe, California and now Cleveland, Tennessee. I felt like our relationship was fate.

I had always worked since I was 16 years old and had my own money. I wasn't serious enough about school and decided not to return to college but get a job. I was so broke; I remember selling all my gold jewelry for spending money. My PK boyfriend didn't return to school either. If I could turn back the clock, I would have finished my education getting my degree in psychology. But at the age of 19, I already knew everything, so I thought. So I got a job working at a local credit union.

My boyfriend lived out of state at the time and came to see me one weekend. I wasn't living right doing things that I knew was wrong. I kept my eyes on man. Knowing that I was not pleasing God, (I didn't talk to Him very often) and I was getting farther and farther away from Him. I would go to church because that's what you do on Sundays. I've done it all my life. I would see the same people I saw at the bar on Saturday night on Sunday raising their hands they were God's best friend. I thought if they could party all week and love God on Sundays that I could do the same. I didn't know God, but He knew me, and I wasn't right. I was pushing God so far from me that I started developing an attitude of, I don't care. Down deep, I knew I needed a Savior. I was raised under the anointing. I knew better than the life style I was living, but I had disappointed myself yet not even knowing who I was. I just knew I didn't like what I had become. I would look in the mirror with disgust, pulling at my hair because I wasn't pretty enough. I was fat. Ever since I was 13 years old I had to deal with a weight issue. One time in Europe (when I was about 12 years) old it was early in the morning, and I was starving for Fritos chips. I decided my mom wouldn't catch me and I would sneak down stairs and grab a few chips. So I sneaked down stairs, went into the walk-in closet, opened the bag of chips that I was craving and the next thing I knew the door was shut and I was locked in the dark closet. Much to my surprise, my mom opened the door and said, "Gottcha." I was so embarrassed. We laugh about that now. Food was always my enemy. I wanted to be picture-perfect thin. I thought that if I was real thin then I wouldn't lose my boyfriend and he would like me more. I would binge eat. I was never consistent with diets. Now I understand that I needed to completely change my way of thinking about food. One night I was so disgusted with my weight I took 16 laxatives at one time thinking that would help me become thinner. When all of the laxatives started moving, no joke intended, all those laxatives at one time ate the lining of my stomach. To this day I have a hard time with my stomach and all that goes with it, if you can read between the lines. That became my way of living. The decisions regarding how you treat your body will affect you for a lifetime.

4

My parents were praying parents. They would do anything for me and help me out in whatever situation I would find myself. I knew they were interceding for me during these difficult times. They began to see me drastically change in every aspect of my life, all because I wanted man's approval. I wanted to impress my boyfriend so I would do things that he did to make him happy so he wouldn't leave me but love me. I was disillusioned. At parties I would get stoned and become so convicted that I would cry thinking Jesus was going to come and I would be left behind. I would try to convince everyone in the room to accept Jesus. The Holy Spirit was always calling me to a deeper place in Him, but I didn't know how to reach Him. His voice was getting fainter and fainter. Satan's grip was getting tighter and tighter. My sister came out to visit us and I recall her asking me the question, "Who is going to pay the rent on this house when Jesus comes and you are left behind?" I was so scared. I would close my eyes hoping and praying Jesus wouldn't come that night. I truly wanted to change, but I thought I was too deep in the sinking sand no one could help me.

In our denomination my father was over 17 nations in Africa. He would travel oversees for long periods of time. One time in particular I received a letter from him. He never really wrote to me but would send me post cards from all the countries and places he would travel. My daddy loved me. This letter was different. It was a prophetic warning letter from God. The letter stated that if I didn't turn from my particular life style I would bare a child out of wedlock - a warning saturated in love. When he returned from this particular trip, I was very sick. Silently, we both knew that the warning would become the truth. I would just shake it off like it was a kidney infection until one day while at work I threw up in the garbage can. The next day I went to the health department. They drew blood and confirmed that I was pregnant. From the age of 16 to 19, I went with unprotected sex thinking it would never happen to me. I thought I was going to die. The words of my father were rehearsed in my mind over and over again. I was in such a devastated mindset that suicide seemed to be my only companion and friend. What am I going to do I thought? My sin has been exposed. I was in denial. I couldn't believe it! I was the slut of the family. I called one of my friends, (who was a preacher's kid too) who I partied with and asked her if she knew a place to get an abortion.   She did so she called and made me an appointment on a Sunday morning of all days, in Atlanta, April of 1983.

One day when I came home, there was a strange car in the yard. I walked through the door and my mom, dad and a counselor friend of the family was sitting in the living room. I entered the living room and my daddy said, "Please come in and sit down so we can talk for a few minutes." When we were little, we would have what was called, King's court. My maiden name is King.   When King's court was announced, it would be a time that we would discuss the troubles in the family and King's court seemed to be such an appropriate name. King's court was really troubled this time. My daddy started off by opening up by explaining that the family had been under stress for several years. The time had come for the motto; "true confession is good for the soul," one more time. I began to cry and confess my heart. I never acknowledged the seed within me was a baby.   I never acknowledged the child within me had a heartbeat, eyes, much less a soul. It was a thing to me. I didn't want to

6

bare this burden I brought upon myself. I wanted to destroy it. I felt dirty, ugly, and unworthy to be called my parents' daughter. I felt I was a disgrace to the family. I had humiliated not only my name but also my family's. Who would ever love me now? Here my sister made all the right decisions, and I can't even make one. Life wasn't worth living for me anymore. My experiences of trying to find my identity had only given me a disease to please. Who are you anymore I would ask myself? I began to express to my parents and the counselor what I was feeling and I asked my daddy to please hold me. Sobbing in his arms like a limp baby in her daddy's lap I laid lifeless. The crying seemed like an eternity. I got back into my chair and told them that I had made an appointment to abort this thing within me. It was the first time I even acknowledged that I was having a baby. Daddy looked at me with tears in his eyes and said, "Baby girl, I can't tell you what to do because you are 19 years old and you obviously have made choices on your own. What I will do is, though I don't agree with your decision to abort this child, I will go with you. You can't go by yourself. I can't allow you to experience this pain on your own." At that moment I experienced Jesus in my living room like never before. My daddy was disappointed with my choices but loved me enough to go with me so I wouldn't be alone. Ed King was my Jesus with skin on.

.   For those of you who are struggling with who you are and what your future holds know this that Jesus will stick closer than a brother to you the Bible says. He said in this life you will have trouble but he would help us through them all. Perhaps your journey is a lot like mine. Maybe you are a preacher's kid, too, who knows better and lived under such an anointing that you too can't believe you are in the situation you are in. Let me reassure you, God is with you. He has a purpose and a plan for your life Jeremiah 29:11 says, He declares a future for you with hope.

That night was one of many divine appointments in my life. I got up the next morning and called my friend who made the appointment for my abortion and told her to please cancel my appointment. I told my parents that I had changed my mind and they were relieved. On December 14, 1983, I made a great decision. I delivered a beautiful 9lb 10oz baby boy named Brandon.

This was a new beginning for my life. I knew nothing about babies, but what I did know was that now I had a purpose and that was to raise this baby in the honor and reverence of God. Did that mean I didn't make any more mistakes? No. It just meant that I now realized that I was living on what I call borrowed oil, my parents anointing. I had no relationship with Jesus, they did. In Matthew 25, Jesus talks about the parable of five wise virgins and five unwise virgins. The five wise virgins' lamps were full of oil, which represents The Holy Spirit. The five unwise were partying and living life foolishly, a lot like I was. When the bridegroom came to get his bride, the five foolish rushed over to the five wise and wanted some of their oil. I am speaking to you by the Spirit of the Lord. The time has come for you to develop a relationship with Jesus Christ and know Him more than just as a good man or perhaps your parents' Savior. He can become your Savior and your best friend by just asking Him to forgive you of your sins and cleanse you from all unrighteousness. It is time to acknowledge you need His oil. The truth is you need Him more than anything. He can fill the emptiness you long for so desperately. You won't find your satisfaction in another man, but the man from Galilee. Please say this pray with me now. Lord I need you. I need to find myself in you. I don't know who I am anymore. Please come into my heart and forgive me of my sins. Purify my heart, cleanse my mind and my belief system from all the perceptions that man has spoken into my spirit and help me to realize you are all I need to be complete. Show me who you are! Reveal yourself to me! I need you more than the breath I breathe! Make your Word come alive in my spirit. Give me strength to say no to the things that have been a part of my life for so long. Breathe into me a new life, your Spirit. Sing over me your satisfaction and make me just like you. Thank you for never leaving me or forsaking me. Thank you for when I call upon you, you hear my cry. I surrender to you all that I am and ever hope to be. Help me to find my identity in you and you alone.

After saying a prayer much like this one taught me, I was on a new beginning of my identity quest. I knew I didn't want to be what I was, but I didn't know how to get to where I knew I needed to be with Jesus. Jesus became real to me. We were developing a relationship. Brandon taught me how to love myself. I always tell Brandon He saved my life. If I had not had him I don't know where I would be today. What the enemy meant for evil God turned into good. He is no respecter of persons. What He did for me He will do for you.

I am reminded of a story I was once told about a little boy who would get scared at night and see monsters in his closet. One night late in the midnight hour he cried out with fear, "Daddy, daddy, please help me I'm scared." Of course, the daddy ran up the stairs to rescue his son from his distress. The little boy's heart was pounding so hard from his chest. When his daddy entered the room he felt peace enter, too. The daddy said, "Son, you don't have to be afraid, Jesus is right here in the room with you." The little boy responded with, "Well daddy, you sleep up here with Jesus and I'll go down stairs and sleep with mommy."

I know life is scary sometimes and fear seems to be your only companion. But I am always reassured when I read in my Bible what my heavenly Father wrote me, telling me not to be afraid for He is right here with me. Let me encourage you, when fear penetrates your heart and mind, and life seems so overwhelming, cry out to God and He will send you the comforter, the sweet Holy Spirit, to cover you in His protection and perfect peace. My Bible tells me He will never leave me or forsake me. You either!

Later in another chapter you will have an opportunity to meet Brandon and walk down his journey and see what he encountered in his search for his identity. He had to take his mask off too and step out from behind his own humanity to walk into his destiny. No longer will the enemy steal his identity. God is good His mercy endures forever.

One night when I was ministering sharing my testimony a sweet little girl came up to me and wanted prayer. She was adorable. She wore pigtails and had a beautiful, cheery smile. I said, "Do you know how beautiful you are?" She shook her head no. I said, "Who told you, you weren't pretty?" She said, "My daddy did." I pulled her close into my bosom like a mother weeping over a wounded child. My heart was broken for her and we began to cry together. If I could have I would have had her come live with me. Her identity was stolen from her by her father. The only foundation she has right now is disappointment, rejection and a low self-esteem. Self-esteem is the way you feel about yourself. Self-image is the way you see yourself. She sees herself from the perception of her father, ugly and worthless. She will find her identity in the first man who remotely shows her any kind of attention, negative or positive if she doesn't build a foundational relationship with Christ and who He says she is.

God thinks you are beautiful. You were created after His image and likeness. He loved you so much that His son Jesus Christ chose to come to take your place on a rugged cross. That should have been me on that cross. Suffering for my own sins but mercy said no, and Jesus took my place. God is a God of love. He did this for you too. He's not in the heavens with a gavel waiting to hit you on the head if you mess up. If He thought we could be perfect and live life perfectly as His children then we wouldn't need Jesus. We could do it on our own.

Today is a new day for you. You don't have to remain the same. Let me encourage you to find a Spirit-filled church that teaches the revelation of the Word. You have to change your environment and makes new friends. Godly friends. Friends that want to do right in the eyes of the Lord, friends who love God and hate sin.

I want to see you in heaven. When you get there look me up! I know God will help you. The difference between a sinner and the saint is the saint gets back up. Please, never, ever, give up! In the book of Joshua, the Word says for us to stay strong and be of good courage. He continues to write and tell us as I was with Moses so shall I be with you. Stay strong my friend for your kinsmen redeemer lives.

Bethany L. Terry is a true southern girl. A Theology major at Lee University, she plans to continue in ministry wherever God takes her. Bethany is extremely blessed with her parents, brother, sister (at heart), and her two adorable dogs, Coco and Hosanna. She loves dancing, going to Wal-Mart, making people laugh (most of the time at her expense), and gaining wisdom whether it be from books or life lessons. Bethany believes that faith, love and wisdom are the three most important virtues in life!

Chapter Two
Insecurity Blanket

Sure, when you're asked "Who are you in Christ?" the easy answer is, "I'm His child," or "a new creation." But we try to just come up with an answer and most of us don't take the time to really analyze the depth of this most important question. When Sandi asked me to be a part of this amazing ministry, I have to admit, I was baffled as to what I was going to say. I didn't want to just give the "churchy" answer, I wanted to seriously dig deep and find out for myself who I *really* am.

I am a very analytical person (and although I'm blonde and can lack common sense sometimes, I can be very deep). So even though I knew the gist of the meaning of "identity," I decided to look it up in the dictionary. Webster's defines it as: "(1) the state of remaining the same (2) the condition of being itself and not another (3) the sense of self." I also looked it up in a thesaurus and found that other words for "identity" are "personality" and "individuality." I pulled out a few of my favorite quotations from my ever popular "Book O' Quotes," to see what an incredibly smart man by the name of C.S. Lewis had to say about these key words.

"The more we let God take us over, the more truly ourselves we become—because He made us. He invented all the different people that you and I were intended to be. It is when I turn to Christ, when I give up myself to His personality, that I first begin to have a real personality of my own."

"Be sure that the ins and outs of your individuality are no mystery to Him; and one day they will no longer be a mystery to you."

"Until you have given up yourself to Him you will not have a real self."

Now, my mom described it something like, "Your identity changes as you grow and mature. Like, you will always be my daughter, that's *who you are*, but with that, your identity changes. You were once my baby, you are now my teenager and one day you will be my married, adult daughter." So spiritually, as we grow into mature disciples, craving steak instead of baby food to feed us, our identity matures and we grow wiser. Allow me to share with you my identity in its present stage.

God Works in Mysterious Ways...

God has blessed me so much! He's given me two wonderful parents, the best sister anyone could ever imagine and a weird (but wonderful) brother. I've been raised in church my whole life, I guess you could say I was "born under a pew." The Word of God is in my house and even though we're only human, my family is a very virtuous family. I honestly don't know why, but God has protected me from *simple* things that He did not choose to protect some of my friends from. It's not because I'm any better than they are, I guess it's just because God goes the extra mile for those who are willing to go the extra mile for Him. All throughout the Bible God has proven that he is no respecter of persons, but he does play favorites! I know God has a great plan for me, but He also has great plans for my friends. The only difference I can think of between my friends and me is His promise to provide a way of escape when in a tempting situation (1 Corinthians 10:13) and I choose to follow the EXIT sign.

Let me elaborate on "simple" things. I can remember one time (several actually, but one in particular,) where one of my really cute guy friends and I were kind of interested in each other, but were making plans to kiss (make out really) just for the heck of it. We talked about it for at least a month (he was a friend I didn't see that often,) and decided that the next time we saw each other we would go through with the plans we had made. As it turns out, we waited for the perfect opportunity, but right before we ventured off to be alone, he started to miss his ex-girlfriend and that seriously spoiled the mood. You may be thinking *he was just all talk, how convenient for him to start missing his ex.* But trust me, if you'd been in that situation, you would know (like I do,) that it was God! Like I said, there's been several times where I've been in that kind of situation (not just with romantic stuff) where I've made up my mind to do something that well, isn't horrible, but isn't great, and God comes along and changes my mind. Believe me, this boy was F-I-N-E! There was no way anyone but God could have changed my mind.

But, even though I'm not perfect and I do things I shouldn't, I look around at my friends' situations and wonder why God protects me from those situations but allows my friends to get into them all the time. Even though sometimes I don't plan to do the righteous thing, God turns things around and without knowing it (on the surface), I do what I know to be right and I remain true. And in the process, God reveals to me my wrong intention and makes it to where I have the right heart about it. I don't know why He does this, I mean, I know He has plans to use these situations for my good future, filled with hope and prosperity but, if at the very least, He's saving me from heartache and regret. And the more I can stay away from those two things… the better!!!

Is the Blood on *YOUR* Hands?

I will be the first one to admit that I am a <u>very</u> outspoken person and in my 18 years of life I've found that most people don't like that. I tell it like it is, I don't like things sugar-coated and I don't like to beat around the bush. I believe, like Rick Warren says, "The truth will set you free, but at first it may make you miserable." When God gives me a truth I need to give to one of my friends, I've learned to obey. It usually means my friend and I don't talk (in several cases) for months, but I'd rather be in trouble with them than with God. I remember plenty of times begging and pleading (foolishly) with God, "Daddy, come on, You don't know what you're making me do! I can't say this to them! Please don't make me!!!" But, I gritted my teeth, spoke the truth (being as polite as I could), and began a period of silence between my self and that person. One time, I spoke something to one of my best friends (of several years) about his romantic life and that apparently was the last straw for him. Believe it or not, I <u>hate</u> conflict, but two weeks later I said something similar to my other best friend. Needless to say, the same thing happened and I went to bed in tears, depressed and wondering *why in the heck does God make me butt into other people's lives?* My mother (whom, if I swore, I would swear she's an angel,) heard my lament and shared with me the story in Ezekiel about the watchman.

When the watchman sees the enemy coming, he blows the alarm to warn the people. Then if those who hear the alarm refuse to take action - - well, it is their own fault if they die. They heard the warning but wouldn't listen, so the responsibility is theirs. If they had listened to the warning, they could have saved their lives. But if the watchman sees the enemy coming and doesn't sound the alarm to warn the people, he is responsible for their deaths. They will die in their sins but I will hold the watchman accountable. "Now, son of man, I am making you a watchman for the people of Israel. Therefore, listen to what I say and warn them for me. If I announce that some wicked people are sure to die and you fail to warn them about changing their ways, then they will die in their sins, but I will hold you responsible for their deaths. But if you warn them to repent and they don't repent, they will die in their sins, but you will not be held responsible." Ezekiel 33:3-9 (NLT)

In most cases, everything I've said to my friends that God has told me to say, He has justified me in my obedience and they have come to me crying, saying that I was right. I say "in most cases," because God is still working on one's heart... But I encourage you dear friend, be an obedient watchman. "Therefore, listen to what I say and warn them for me."

Dr. Fickle and Mrs. Bride

Like the story of Dr. Jekyll and Mr. Hyde (the famous doctor who turns into a beast), I too have a severe case of split personalities. On the Bride side, I am a sweet, innocent goody-goody whose only problem is her bad attitude sometimes. But on the Dr.'s side, I'm a hypocritical Christian, who preaches one thing yet practices another. I've gotten to the point where I can commit a sin the world would call "innocent," but God lays the conviction on me like I've just committed murder. And honestly, I have, more times than there is a number for. To know that I am responsible for someone's death is the worst feeling ever created. I murdered an innocent, unarmed man, by the name of Jesus Christ. Now, I know you're thinking "come on, give me a break. Pah-leez!" No, I'm serious. I mean this with every fiber of my being. I used this literal analogy to express the seriousness and weight of the matter. Even the tiniest things I do that I know are wrong have the biggest impacts on me. Most recently, I had an impure thought about my boyfriend (at the time). THANK GOD I'm a very sexual being, but also THANK GOD I've not acted upon my sexual desires. No perverted jokes, innuendos, or words were said. Only a lustful thought that grew into an unwanted action that millions of people do everyday and even in the church no one would call me a slut or a skank if they found out. It was just something I would never do in front of my parents. God, in His Almighty righteousness placed upon me His really annoying conviction (this time, a double dose). Needless to say, I felt like the worst person that ever existed, compared to me, I felt Adolph Hitler was a saint. Knowing that I'd never done anything hardly like this, I felt my witness and testimony was ruined. I begged God, "Please just let this be something that I can learn something from. Better yet, let me learn what You would have me learn. Let me learn from my mistakes and let others learn from them too, so they won't have to feel this way, Father. And above all, please just let me make it through this. You work everything to the good of those who love You. I'm waiting! When is this going to pull a 360 and equal the good you've promised? Most of all, I'm hurt and depressed that I was a hypocrite. I mean, I've been hardheaded and strong-willed my entire life. When I say I'm gonna do something, I do it. So why is this any different? Why can't I be strong enough to maintain my Christian witness to my boyfriend, whom I care about so much? Who even though he's a Christian, needs my steadiness as the biggest encouragement to help his walk? Why? Why am I acting like such a loser? Why am I, after 17 ½ years of practicing doing what I say I'm gonna do, going back on my word? Just tell me why! Or better yet, just give me the solution!"

I know I'm human! I know I will make mistakes everyday of my life, but this was a stupid unneeded one. It's like in football (my favorite sport!). The players have played this sport their whole lives, they practice everyday, and they know the rules inside and out. But it never fails, when they're playing the most important game of their lives, they always lose 5 or more crucial yards by simply making a stupid mistake like off-sides, pass interference, or even holding. They've trained basically their whole life not to make those simple mistakes and it ends up happening! I've come to the conclusion that stupidity is a huge part of human nature.

Someday My Prince Will Come… But I Think He Took A Wrong Turn, Got Lost, And Is Too Stubborn To Ask For Directions!

Knowing my history, that is exactly what's happened to my man. O.K., well, maybe not, but it sure seems that way! With all my weaknesses I think guys are my biggest challenge in life, especially when it comes to waiting patiently for the right one. I've been boy crazy since I knew they existed. When I was 5, I would chase my brother's 10 & 11 year old friends around the baseball park because I thought they were so cute! We won't go into my dating history, but I've always been obsessed with the opposite sex. One reason is, my whole life, no matter what I chose to become when I was an adult, I knew the one thing that would never change would be my desire to be a wife. I suppose another reason is Satan knows I would never be stupid enough to get into drugs or alcohol, but knows that I would be extremely tempted with sexual things. I am proud to say that I have remained a virgin (and haven't done anything more than kiss,) my whole life. And I am determined to stay this way until I'm married.

(Back to the prince thing.) Hollywood is notorious for brainwashing us into believing the kind of "love" shown on movies and television. But the truth is you can't have a decent, lasting relationship with stories found in "Pretty Woman" or "Dirty Dancing." But millions of people buy into that lie everyday. No wonder the divorce rate is going up more and more! I'm not just talking about saving yourself (sexually) for when you get married, I'm saying save yourself for the RIGHT one to marry. No one's going to be perfect, but God has created the one to fit you perfectly!

Sandi came to me not too long ago and with many words of encouragement she added, "Don't just wait for the good-man, wait for the God-man!" Meaning, don't just settle for someone you could live with... wait patiently for the one God created *just for you*!!! In the book, "I Kissed Dating Goodbye", a man by the name of John Fischer states,

"God has called me to live now, not four years from now. He wants me to realize my full potential as a man right now, to be thankful for that, and to enjoy it to the fullest. I have a feeling that a single person who is always wishing they were married will probably get married, discover all that is involved, and wish they were single again. A possible question they might ask themselves will be *why didn't I use that time, when I didn't have so many other obligations, to serve the Lord? Why didn't I give myself totally over to Him then?*"

I'm convinced that if we all lived by that policy, we'd find contentment in our singleness and if we would wait for marriage and our God-mate, the divorce rate would plummet. We need to learn to openly receive our single years (however numerous they might be) as a gift, instead of grudgingly accept them out of obligation as a curse. Like I said, it's my biggest challenge, but I am trying and day by day improving.

Here is another letter I wrote in my desperation:
"O.K., I may only be 17 but it seems like my prince will never come. I know I need to sit back and wait, but it seems like I have to wait an eternity for him. I realize this, but I need to believe it and keep remembering that the wait is a huge part of it. It's about the destination, yes, but without the journey you have no way of getting there. Without the journey, we'd all stay where we started from forever. Without the wait, you can't truly appreciate the gift. When you reach the destination and find each other there, then you'll have something to talk about on your next journey together toward the next destination God puts in your life. Someday my prince will come... but why are men such procrastinators?

What will he look like? How scrumptious will he smell? Will I melt when I see his smile? But the most important question to me right now is when is he going to get here??? God, please answer me soon. Better yet, just *bring* him to me and soon!!!"

I must share a story that has encouraged me in my wait for my prince. One Sunday morning in our IBC (Interactive Bible Class), a wonderful, attractive, 22 year old man named Jonny told of his effort to wait patiently for his bride. He said, "I have this empty picture frame in my room and every time I get lonely or discouraged I look at it and think, *God, I know you haven't brought her into the picture yet, but I know you will. So until that day, I wait for Your promise to be fulfilled.*" Needless to say, every girl in the class was crying because of the sweetness and romance of Jonny's heart, not to mention his commitment to walk in obedience and wait. So, of course, I went the next day and bought an empty picture frame that sits right across from my bed so I see it each night before I go to sleep! Fellas and ladies, just be encouraged in your wait, because somewhere, your bride or your prince is waiting for you! And if by chance they *do* take a wrong turn, get lost and are too stubborn to ask for directions (like my man ha, ha), don't worry, God will place them on the road that leads straight to your arms!

But, as I am doing, take this time to find your faults and fix them. Because God deserves your best and so does the other love of your life!

Mirror, Mirror, On The Wall

Although it may seem that Snow White is just an entertaining fairytale, we can use its moral and apply it to our own life, because for a lot of us we identify all too well with the story (even if we don't know it). I don't mean we sing and dance with the cute forest creatures or live in a cottage with 7 whistling, short, old guys. I mean, how we are fed lies our entire lives about who we are.

In this Walt Disney film, there is an attractive princess who is not only beautiful on the outside, but on the inside as well. Then, there is an evil queen, who is consumed by jealousy for the beautiful princess. And for the sake of this story, lastly, we have the magic mirror on the wall that is, shall I say, more on the good side since it cannot lie. But, when it comes to you and me in the *real* world, the mirror is more like the wicked queen. In our world (for those of you who are like I was and sometimes am), we look in the mirror and no matter what our reflection, we see something upsetting.

As Sandi would say she had a disease to please people, I had a disease to please the mirror. It got to where I would cry sometimes if I had to look in a mirror to fix my hair or check my mascara. Like the evil queen, I could never please the mirror. But unlike the story, where the mirror tells the truth, in reality it is incapable of telling anything other than lies. And we listen to its lies everyday instead of looking at ourselves with the eyes of our Father.

In this fairytale, the queen is ruled by jealousy, greed and insecurity. So much that she will do <u>whatever</u> it takes to destroy her competition. At first she starts by going for the princess's mind. Brainwashing her to believe all she is worthy of are the rags given to her out of pity by the queen. Sound familiar…? And for the most part, her evil plan works, seeing as how Snow White was very embarrassed for Prince Charming to see her in her rags. For those who haven't figured it out yet, the Queen (and the mirror in reality) represents Satan, Snow White represents us, and Prince Charming ("PC" as I like to say,) represents our JC (Jesus Christ). Well, the fear of rejection by the Prince lasts only a moment. She is then taken over by the love she has for the Prince and His love for her, and let's go of her insecurities. This is very upsetting to the arrogant queen, and makes her afraid and vulnerable. She realizes that if the princess and prince marry, then her kingdom is doomed.

Once Satan knows he can't have your mind anymore, he then goes for your life. Maybe it's not your physical life, maybe it's your mental, or spiritual. But whatever the case is, he seeks to put an end to it. Just like the queen sending out a huntsman to kill the princess and bring back her heart.

Now, I won't go through the whole story, because we all know how it ends. The evil queen is destroyed and good prevails. Just like the ending in the Bible (of course I still haven't figured out where the dwarves fit in…).

But to share my Snow White connection… I have always had much insecurity when it comes to my physical appearance. I have many people tell me that I'm beautiful, but like Julia Roberts said in Pretty Woman, "The bad stuff is easier to believe." And I have found that to be quite true. Nonetheless, the enemy uses my mirror on the wall or <u>any</u>

mirror to lie to me. He gets in my mind and makes me feel <u>so</u> insecure, especially around other girls. Now, do I know the lies I believe to be true? Absolutely not! I believe God's word to be true, but, to my human mind, the lies are more logical. They make more sense than a God who doesn't make mistakes. How can I associate imperfection with being perfect? When in my mirror I see physical "imperfections" (too short, acne, ugly feet, etc...). How can this be God's ideal of being perfect? God does <u>not</u> make mistakes, so how can I transform myself into being secure and content? It is a simple answer with a profound truth, by renewing my mind. And like I've said many times, I'm trying my hardest to live the truth and little by little improving. And like every story has a beginning, middle and end, I'm in the center and waiting for my Happily Ever After with my true prince charming, Jesus Christ!

Fake I.D.

My heart weeps every time I think about a dear friend of mine. He was adopted when he was just a baby, and that started his life off in total confusion. I can only imagine the feelings of rejection and not knowing where you belong that come with being adopted. His adopted parents are wonderful people but the relationship the three of them share has never been great. Unfortunately, his whole 18 years, my friend has had a bigger void in his life than I have, but like every single human, he has looked in all the wrong places for something to fill that void. I weep because of how much I cherish him, but weep even more because I know most people in the world are in his same situation. On the outside they think they know who they are, but on the inside (behind the mask) they are desperately searching for their true identity.

I believe that identity and peace go hand in hand. Peace (true peace) comes from knowing who you are, and that is why my dear friend is living a life of struggle. Most people who have not found their identity will eventually become so desperate they will look *anywhere* to find it (anywhere but the right place). They will rush into drinking, smoking, drugs, sexual relationships and anything else that is only temporary. Just ask Sandi. But like *all* things temporary, eventually the fix wears off (hence the label "temporary") and the void is still there. A lot of times the emptiness even grows because they think they've filled it but their plan doesn't work. So they go back time after time, getting deeper into sin as the vicious cycle continues. Until they find the truth (if they ever do), they continue living in zombie mode, struggling to get by with a fake I.D.

One of my favorite truths is, "If you always do what you've always done, then you'll always get what you've always got." Now, I have never gotten sucked into the *severe*, vicious identity cycle, because I chose to listen to that truth. When I realize something isn't working, I like to find something that will. My prayer is that everyone who is looking to things that aren't working and will never work, to fill their emptiness will just turn around to see God with His loving hands extended, holding peace that will *never* fade. It's that easy! If you're looking for peace and nothing is working, just look over your shoulder. I give you a money back guarantee that true peace (that has a lifetime warranty) will catch your attention, and keep it.

More Romantic Than Romeo and Juliet

As I mentioned earlier, I have grown severely impatient waiting for my prince. But over the past year, patience has nudged its way into my life and become part of my identity. I didn't decide to give up on him; I just decided to "give him time to become more romantic" (ha, ha). I have written letters to him for years and will continue to do so until the day I die. It is a way for me to have him with me without *having* him with me. It's therapeutic for the lonely days, and just in case we get bored on our honeymoon (which won't happen) he'll have plenty to read. Plus, I know it will warm his heart and let him know even when I didn't know who or where in the world he was, I thought of him constantly. I am completely in love with him and don't even know who he is. I know of quite a few people who have chosen not to date until God brings them their husband/wife and I am doing the same. Although we haven't officially begun our relationship, our bond is already amazingly strong. The reason why... I am in love with someone else.

I got your attention there didn't I? Like I was saying, I have fallen head over heels for the Lover of my soul. For the longest time I've looked at Sandi's relationship with Father and have wanted that kind of passion but never thought that was my style of intimate relationship with Him. But since I've started trusting Him with *everything* it is seriously like we are engaged to be married. This may sound like a silly little girl fantasy, but, I was driving down the road one evening and saw this incredible sunset (I LOVE sunsets)! It was bright with pinks, oranges, and purples and absolutely breathtaking. I finally realized the One who has my heart painted that *just* for me! He paints the sky each day just to see me smile. I never thought of God as a romantic, but He *created* romance. Wow! Then, I was driving home after dark and saw hundreds of fireflies putting on a lightshow for me. It looked like twinkling Christmas lights scattered throughout the open field. I knew that Father orchestrated their performance just to bring joy to my heart. It is kind of like, your best friend whom you have never noticed romantically, has been doing his best to win your heart for years, and one day, you finally realize he's the one for you. You even begin to notice every single thing he used to do and continues to do every day to make you smile. All He wants is our love and I've been a fool not to give it to Him like He desires. All I want is to make Him smile any way I can, now that I finally get it.

I told you that I write letters to my future husband, but I never said I also write letters to the Lover of my soul. If you haven't written letters to the man/woman you are going to marry, I encourage you to do so. It will comfort you when you're lonely or discouraged and it will mean the world to them once they have become your husband/wife and they have the privilege of reading them. But, let me also encourage you to write letters to the One who formed you in your mother's womb. Even though He knows exactly what you're thinking, it still means so much to Him, whether it is a cry of insanity or a declaration of your love for Him. Plus, it soothes your spirit and years down the road you can look back and see where you were and how far you've come. Not only that, but you can have a reminder of how faithful our Lover is. I wrote this letter, in poetic form, to Father about my romantic sunset encounter with Him.

My Lover painted a sunset for me this evening. It was an amazing sunset full of brightly colored pinks and oranges. It lit up the sky like He lights up my heart. But this was no painting on an ordinary canvas, for my Lover's canvas is the sky itself! His beautiful masterpiece was a declaration of His love for me. As I drove home, my attention was caught by the incredible serenade of fireflies beaming their lights in perfectly beautiful timing. While I traveled deeper into the wood, their performance dazzled me and beckoned me to dance with my Beloved. I was mesmerized by His love for me and by the romance in His thoughtful gifts. He once again showed how He wins my heart day by day. Satisfying my heart's desires above and beyond, even the ones I never knew existed. My Lover is the hero of my dreams and the Love of my life!

Just A Little Encouragement

Ephesians 6:12 states, "For our struggle is not against flesh and blood, but against the rulers, against the authorities, against the powers of this dark world and against the spiritual forces of evil in the heavenly realms" (NIV). And in the Message Bible, "This is no afternoon athletic contest that we'll walk away from and forget about in a couple of hours. This is for keeps, a life-or-death fight to the finish against the Devil and all his angels." Guys, this is the biggest battle of our lives! Don't just conquer, but overcome your struggles, weaknesses and insecurities. I pray you will be encouraged not to give up or give in. I'm fighting this battle with you, and better yet, so is our Father!

High Tech Security System

My whole life I have carried around a dirty, ragged, nasty, old blanket called Insecurity. The need I felt to have that blanket clutched in my hand at all times was caused by the desire I had to control my life, past, present, and future. I knew things would eventually crumble and fall since I have serious limits as an imperfect human being. Once I understood, believed, and trusted that only Father could handle such a task (and beautifully I might add,) and I surrendered everything (including my heart and heart's desires) into His hands, I traded in my insecurity blanket for a beautiful, majestic, garment of peace, hope and most of all, security. Like a fugitive who is running from the law, searching frantically for a place to hide, surrenders to the police, so must we surrender to our Father. The cool thing is, once we surrender, we don't get thrown in a dark, cold, lonely cell; we get wrapped in our Daddy's comfy robe, sit at His table while we feast on delicious yummies, and bask in the relaxation of His enormous mansion! So what are you waiting for? Get out the white flag!!!

<u>That's All Folks!</u>

These are just a few stories and characteristics that make up God's little girl. I would say this is the end of the story, but I can't. I'm glad the story isn't over, I'm glad your identity changes as you grow and mature. I'm also glad that I've followed C.S. Lewis' wisdom, that we don't have a real self or even a real identity until we fully give ourselves over to Christ. Thankfully, I have already done that, or otherwise I wouldn't have been able to write this chapter because I wouldn't have a true identity. Finally, I'm so thankful God gives me chance, after chance, after chance to improve myself. I'm thankful for trials and tribulations that test my faith and develop perseverance, so my identity may eventually be mature and <u>complete</u> not lacking anything! (James 1:2-4 NIV)

May the God of peace be with you always. Amen.

30

Mario Hood majors in Christian Ministry with an emphasis in Bible. Since he was saved in 2002, he continually finds himself growing through the knowledge of the Word. Mario plans to pursue a Masters in Divinity after the completion of his bachelor's. He plans to use his education to minister to the lost and one day plant a church. He and his wife's heartbeat resemble a passion for seeing the people of our inner cities restored, revived and released into their God ordained destiny. Mario enjoys playing sports, quality time with his wife, and playing with his dogs. His testimony is one of many that prove our God's grace is limitless and His loves will never know failure.

Chapter Three
Reality

"Reality is the sum of all that is real, absolute and unchangeable." For me reality began on November 10, 2002, just after my 18th birthday. I know what you're thinking; how can someone be living for 18 years without being in reality? Well, this is my story it all began October 25, 1984.

Birth: Into This Physical World

I, Demario Dequan Hood, was born in Greenville, SC. I joke about it now and say I was born trying to walk in my destiny because I tried to come out feet first, or maybe I was just trying to be difficult. God blessed my mother with two gifts, and I was the second one, being born a year and nine months later than my older brother, Donques. Growing up so close in age, my brother and I were inseparable. To say the least, it wasn't easy for a single mother to raise two kids especially two males. There are only so many things a woman can show two growing men, but we made it and I look back and know it was by God's mercy and grace that we did. I don't regret anything that happened as a child growing up, but I look at it as the landscape in which God paints the perfect picture. When all is said and done just remember if you're not comfortable with your past you'll never conform to your future.

The Life I Knew

When you think about the word family, a picture of a mom and a dad with their two kids, living in their big house with a white picket fence usually comes to mind. More often than not this is the picture portrayed in the media, and according to that standard who could live up to that? My family was anything but perfect. First there was no dad, just my mom, my brother and me, and second my brother and I have different dads. My family also includes my two cousins, my aunt and my grandmother. We are a tight knit group and nobody from the outside can affect the bond we have, but the problems were not external but internal.

Growing up I thought my family was the only one with problems. I mean my friends always seemed happy with their family situation. It's funny how the enemy likes to get you to think that you are the only one in a certain situation. Loneliness sets in, depression takes over, and if the enemy can get you to feel alone then he's got you in a fatal position. The Bible says in Deuteronomy and in Joshua, "God will never leave us nor forsake us". I know it's a Scripture which people quote a lot, but I dare you to really think about what this verse is really crying out. God says, in Psalms 139, no matter the circumstances, no matter the situation, He will always be there, even if you make your bed in hell, Jesus will be right their beside you. I knew a man, who was once a murderer, in fact his job was to go find Christians and kill them, but one day God set him up for a divine encounter and his life was changed forever, his name was Paul, and if God can change his situation then God can change yours.

Lost and Lonely

At the age of nine, my mother thought it would be best if my brother and I went to a school that was a home for children. A home for children is an orphanage for children and is usually operated by a particular church denomination. The home for children that we were placed in was called; Thornwell Home and School for Children and it was run by the Presbyterian Church.

The Home doubled as a private school that anyone could attend hence the name 'home and school', thus it enabled kids that were not living in the home to attend school in the daytime and they were called day-schoolers. On the flipside the kids who lived in the home and did not have the privilege to go home to their parent(s) every night, were known as residents, all together there were about one hundred to one hundred and twenty-five kids at the home and school.

Living in the home (the residents) meant that you could only see your parent(s) every other weekend that is after you went through a trial period of three months of no personal visits just phone calls and letters. Of course being in an orphanage some kids didn't have parents at all and had been living in the home since birth, but I can remember one set of brothers that only got to see their family at major holidays because they lived so far away.

At the home it was sort of an unwritten rule that when you first got to Thornwell, you had to tell why you had been placed in the home. Most of the kids were there because they had no mother or father, some were put there because the state took them from their parent(s), and others were there because their parent(s) said they were out of control and could not handle them. When I got to Thornwell I avoided this question because I really had no idea why my mom put us there. From what I was told it was because my brother's grandmother was a worker there, known as a houseparent. But as the kids continued to come and all had 'major' reasons why they were, like no parents or the state took them from their parents for various reasons. As this scenario happen over and over again, the question formed in my mind, what was the real reason that my mom put us here? Eventually the truth would come out and she told us that she could not fully provide for us. That it was difficult for her as a single parent with no concrete job to feed three mouths. That the constant moving every six months was not good for growing kids because they had no friends. Life was just too hectic for her and she made the hard decision to place her two boys in the Home.

Looking back at the time that was spent at Thornwell, in the light of my testimony, I never fail to mention that putting my brother and me in the home was the best parenting decision that my mom has ever made. When I first got to Thornwell I was so young in age that all I could think was that my mom was giving my brother and me away. I went from seeing her everyday to twice a month, and it was such a hard adjustment. I remember crying almost every night the first month we were separated. The only thing that kept me going was the sure fact that my brother was there with me. Once a month we had to go see a counselor who asked us these question about my mom like if I thought she loved us and do you ever feel angry at your mom. It was so embarrassing, so after the first visit I called home to my mother and complained and told her, but we still continued to go for three months. My whole life was turned upside down, and I felt that everything I knew and understood about life was crashing down on top of me.

After the three-month trial period things began to get better and I would later realize the benefits of the situation. I realized that when I lived with my mom we were moving every four to six months, which meant that keeping the same friends was out of the questions. While I was at Thornwell, I could wake up everyday knowing that my best friend, James, was going to be there. My mom would have never been able to pay for me to go on hiking or camping trips or pay for me to attend basketball or baseball camps, now at Thornwell I could. Being at Thornwell it allowed me to experience things that a young black kid from the streets could only dream about. As I look back I am also reminded of the verse, "For I know the plans I have for you declares the Lord, plans to prosper you not to harm you, plans to give you a hope and a future." God used Thornwell to plant a seed in my mind and spirit that there was more out there than what the world was about to offer me, and God had a plan for my life from the very beginning. Notice I said about, because little did I know that my brother and I were about to leave the place we had grown so familiar with.

Slave to Sin

Thornwell was a Presbyterian based home and for five years they had sown the Word of God into my spirit and opened my mind to a higher calling. That calling would be harvested after a four-year drought and then a quick storm. John 8: 34 says, "Assuredly anyone who commits sin is a slave to sin." The summer between my eighth-grade year and freshman year of high school my brother and I were sent back to live with my mother. I have never admitted it until now but I had mixed feelings of going to live with my mother. The friends I had known for five years were suddenly getting ready to disappear and transform into memories. I was about to start all over again. I can remember crying from the time I left Thornwell until the time we reached our apartment in Anderson, SC (about 2 hour drive).

Anderson was a new world to me after being in Thornwell for five years. It was almost as if I had been in a box and suddenly dumped out. In Thornwell I was sheltered from drugs, alcohol, and sexual things. The boys and girls at Thornwell dated and maybe kissed but that was certainly it. Now I was thrown back into a lifestyle that I had forgotten all about as a kid.

Being a freshman at a new school, I wanted to make friends and make them any way I could. One of the ways I thought I could make friends was to try out for the junior varsity basketball team. As football season passed and basketball tryouts were coming up, I had made few friends and I was hoping that I would make the team and make friends. To my luck or maybe skills I made the team and friends. Two of the guys would become my new best friends.

I also made friends through trying the party scene. Everybody wants to try the party scene in high school. By the end of my freshman year I had begun to drink on the weekends. Within one year of leaving Thornwell, I had already fallen into temptation. By the end of my sophomore year I had begun to smoke marijuana on the weekends, while I still played basketball. I had all the friends I wanted, especially since they could come to my house and smoke and drink all they wanted. The only catch was that they had to share with my bother, me and sometimes mom. My mom believed that if we were going to do drugs and drink alcohol, we might as well do it where she could supervise. In the lifestyle of sin it all made sense, but God has called us to be holy and abstinent from worldly things.

My junior year only became worse. I smoked daily and still drank on the weekends. By my senior year I had quit the basketball team and was drinking, smoking and popping pills almost everyday. I had truly become a slave to sin, with no way out or so I thought. Sin has a way of creeping into your life and taking over your life before you even realize it. By the time you do realize it maybe one, five, or twenty years later, but how gracious is our God to care so much for His people.

Divine Appointment

Sin crept into my life and almost completely took over. Before I knew it the end of my senior year was approaching. The pressure of my whole life was to be the one who would succeed in my family. It began to over take me and it snatched me out of a tailspin long enough for me to focus on getting into college. Most high school students start filling out their stuff for college in their junior year or even their senior year, but I waited until one month before college was about to start. I had no idea what to do, but I went to someone who did, God.

One of my best friends from the basketball team had gone to college a year earlier and told me about this Christian school called Lee University. He loved the school and made it sound great, but how could I ever go to a Christian school that made the freshmen have a 12:00 am curfew and go to church (chapel) every Tuesday and Thursday morning. But the option was to go to college here or nothing at all. You would be surprised at the choice you make when you are desperate and I desperately wanted to go to college and not be stuck in the "hood" for life and become another statistic.

Now you have to understand my spiritual state at the time, I was not saved, matter of fact I had not prayed or gone to church in four years ever since I left Thornwell, but I can clearly remember saying in my bed, "Lord, if you can get me into Lee University then I will give up all this junk for you." Little did I know what God had in store for me.

Miracle 1: When There Was No Way, He Made A Way

The first miracle that I recognized God performed was that I was accepted into college. I didn't even take the ACT until I arrived on the campus not to mention filling out all the paper work and financial aid documents a month before classes started. My roommate was my other best friend from high school. I truly did thank God, but soon after reading the acceptance letter, the prayer I prayed had been lost in the inner banks of my memory. My mind was set on living the college life and it flipped right back to sex, drugs and alcohol. Yes, even at a "Christian" school.

Miracle 2: The Virtuous Woman

The second miracle God performed was that he set me up for what I call "our divine appointment." I said "our" because I am talking about the first time my soon-to-be wife and I ever met. As I mentioned before, after being accepted my lifestyle of sin suddenly found a way to creep back in. All I could think about was going back to that lifestyle of sin. It's amazing how we quickly forget the things God has done for us. Before I had the chance to sink deep into the pits of sin again, I was due for an 18 year appointment.

Classes started on a Wednesday, but on a Monday one of the fraternities held a "Welcome Back Party" on campus and I was just hanging out with the boys, trying to meet girls. That night I met a girl that I would never forget. Believe me when I say, it was love at first sight. From the moment I saw her I was instantly drawn to her and I knew that there was something different about this one. Trying to play it cool I casually introduced myself and she told me her name was Megan. From that moment on I knew I had to have her, and as I look back now I know I was drawn to the anointing of God on her life.

Reality Hits

For the next few months Megan and I became friends. I wasn't looking to rush into a relationship and especially not my freshman year of college. I remember knowing that we were at that point of deciding if we would be friends or become boyfriend and girlfriend and start dating. As this point approached she assuredly let me know that I had some things that I needed to allow God to deal with.

I will never forget that Sunday night we were sitting outside my dorm and she told me that she would never date me if I stayed in the spiritual state I was in. I was shocked and completely appalled that she would say my lifestyle was "wrong." I grew up in that lifestyle. Cussing, drinking, and using drugs was the normal way of life for me. I thought to myself, who is she to say that I am wrong and she is right? I told her that we wouldn't date then because I wasn't ready to give this lifestyle up. I was young I was supposed to be having fun.

As soon as I got out of her car, conviction set in and stayed with me for almost one whole week. On Thursday, the campus was in its fourth night of convocation, a weeklong revival with a night service every night, the speakers name was Lorain Livingston and he preached his socks off. I knew God was speaking to me through him and the conviction was unbearable. He asked the students to give up three things for God, things that were hindering us from God. I made the decision to give up drinking, smoking and cussing. A burden was truly lifted off my shoulders. I couldn't wait to tell Megan what I had just experienced.

Miracle 3: Delivered from Strongholds

I went back to my dorm and told Megan to meet me there because I had something to tell her. We sat right outside my dorm and I told her everything that had happened. I could tell in her eyes she was happy but still reluctant to fully trust me in that way. A short amount of time later we started dating and I can truthfully say that I have never struggled with drinking, smoking or cussing again.

Miracle 4: Revelation of Reality

Megan would frequently ask me to go to church with her and I always said, no. I came up with every excuse to say no and just when I thought I had run out I would create another one. Finally, I ran out and made the choice to go, man was God really setting me up. Jesus says "If you lift Me up then I will draw all men unto Me" (John 12:32) and Megan had done just that. She had sought his face until he had no choice but to answer her prayer. As soon as I stepped in the church I knew why I had avoided the place for so long, it was a service for middle school kids. Man, I couldn't wait to get out of there. I thought to myself I will never come back.

We arrived late and it was my fault. After service I met the pastors of the middle school ministry. They were cool people from the Bronx. They knew my lifestyle and from the first time I met them they made me feel welcome. I went back week after week not really knowing why but I had to keep going because something was pulling at my heart.

A short time later, my life would change forever because my world would be turned upside down again making it right-side up. November 10, 2002, I was saved and reality hit, and I found my own identity, my true identity in Christ. It wasn't by crying or falling out but by a simple prayer that made a huge statement. For 18 years, I searched for ways to express myself. Was I an orphan because I grew up at an orphanage? Was I just a jock because I played sports in high school? Or was I the stereotype black kid in the hood that sold drugs? Was I a slave to sin because I couldn't control the urges of my flesh? Finally, I had the answer and it was none of the above. I wasn't an orphan because I serve a God who is a Father to the fatherless (Psalm 68:5). He is Jehovah Jireh, the one who looks after all of us. I could no longer be stereotyped as the jock or drug dealer who would have no life after high school because Jeremiah 29:11 became so evident in my life. I was and am a living, breathing, walking testimony of His miraculous power. Though I was a slave to sin Romans 6:6 says, "That the old self has been crucified with him so that the body of sin might be done away with." Paul teaches that as God frees us from sin we should become slaves to righteousness.

The truth is that reality is the spiritual world not the one we live in. We should define ourselves according to that. The Bible says that our lives are but a vapor in time (James 4:14). Why live for the world? We are supposed to be in the world but not of the world. Paul says to set your hope on heavenly things, eternal things. If you lack God in your identity it will not last forever, because we where created in his image (Genesis 1:27). Every person on the face of the earth is seeking to find out who he or she is and where he or she came from.

I started this chapter by defining in words what reality is: the sum of all that is real, absolute and unchangeable, and I will end it with a portrait; Jesus Christ on the cross, without it our true identity would be lost forever.

Megan Hood is a student attending Lee University studying Psychology. With the completion of this degree, she will pursue her calling in Inner City Ministry, as she walks alongside her husband doing the Lord's work. Megan hopes to further her education in professional counseling and studying marriage and family therapy. She enjoys spending time with her family, photography and chasing after her two lively puppies. She loves to write and hopes to one day create her own greeting card line. She believes the possibilities in her future are limitless with the blessings of Jesus Christ and hopes to mother children someday and reach millions through counseling, writing and preaching.

Chapter Four
Puzzled

If there is one thing in life I despise, its puzzles. All the way back in second grade I remember missing recess because I wouldn't complete a crossword puzzle. Anything that has the word puzzle in it, I run the other way. My mom, on the other hand, loves them. I've tried to express the dizzy nauseating feeling I get in my head when I attempt one, but she says I am only exaggerating. I know why I hate them so much. It's because there is always a piece missing or a piece that seems to fit but doesn't fit comfortably enough, causing an unattractive bulge that distorts the image of the puzzle. Shamefully my life has reflected a puzzle; misshapen or incomplete.

Genesis, the creation, must have been the very first puzzle ever created. In the first chapter of Genesis we are told all the things God created. This process took six days. At different times with various, yet few words spoken, this earth was crafted together piece by piece, perfectly. Yet even in the creation process, a piece was missing. That piece was finally created and became woman. Adam and Eve, you and I were created from the dirt of the ground (Genesis 2:7).

Looking back at what my puzzle once was, makes me thankful that I serve a God who cared enough for me to step into my broken heart and confused mind and reveal to me a plan and future (Jeremiah 29:11). I was in church all of my life, and I was always very involved. I began to teach two-year old Sunday school at the young age of fifteen. I began working youth camps and teaching Wednesday night classes for middle schoolers. When I was a senior in high school, I was given the opportunity of a lifetime to work with middle schoolers. For a number of years in my life I was helping so many people allow God to put their puzzles together, but mine was so incomplete and misshapen. I needed God to transform me from dirt to a beautiful garden that bore not the things of the flesh but things of the Spirit. Why was I so lifeless and without His joy? Because I lacked the concept that everything in life will fade and fail you, but He is the foundation that will never lack strength.

The Glass House

The enemy has such a way of taking positive things and making them negative. He uses tactics that can confuse you so quickly, if you aren't in the Word! I was blessed with two parents who loved me and provided for me since I took my first breath. My parents wanted so badly to shield me from evil and smother me in virtuous environment. They did the best they could have done, but there is a point in everyone's life where you must decide for yourself where your faith will reside. The Bible talks of loving nothing or anyone more than Him and His plans for you.

My father is a minister and he does a great deal of traveling. God has given him a mighty vision and burden for families. He coordinates family ministries and helps restore lifeless marriages. My dad held a position in which he was on call twenty-four hours a day. His office was connected to an answering service and if a minister had a crisis in the middle of the night, their call was then transferred to our house. My dad was awakened many times in the night to counsel hurting people. Sometimes my whole family was awakened due to the phone ringing. I began praying. God, there are two things I never want you to call me to; the ministry and a 24-hour hotline.

Growing up as a preacher's kid wasn't easy. Growing up with a father who was an expert on families and who traveled the world trying to bring hope to families and marriages on the verge of breaking up was unbearable. The enemy deceived me into thinking I had to be perfect and what wasn't perfect was to be kept silent behind closed doors. I can remember talking to my dad a few times about things that troubled me and he guided me and counseled me the best he knew how. Though I knew I had parents who loved me, I felt a big wall between us a lot. I believe almost every teenager feels this way. I heard a student who recently graduated from seminary say it well, "I am called to ministry and so is my whole family. The difference between my children's calling and my calling is I have the choice to answer that calling, they don't."

Dad and I are a lot alike. I couldn't deny him if I ever wanted to. We look exactly alike. I always wondered what he would think if I confessed to feeling a certain way or messing up in certain areas. I felt as though I had a multitude of "dirty little secrets" hidden inside, secrets of feelings and questions. I allowed the enemy to transform our beautiful 4 bedroom and 4 bathroom home into a house. He tricked me into thinking the roof over my head was just a few walls and was not safe. I was in a house but not a home.

As I grew older, I became confused and tormented with thoughts of failure. I hated who I was and what I looked like. I felt like I was living in a glass house for everyone to see in. I felt like a showcase that acted like a programmed robot saying all the right things in front of the right people. The problem was I didn't care who liked me, loved me or what anyone thought about me. I felt like reputation and presentation of yourself was everything to the people around me. I was as pleasant as I could be, but when the lights went out, I wept myself to sleep many nights.

I felt like no one knew me, for me. I was always John and Su's daughter or Meredith and Mel's little sister. There was so much inside of me that I felt was overlooked. I was just a dusty figurine, showcased behind walls of glass for everyone to see.

Desiring to be Desired

As I began high school, my body began changing. I was tall and very thin. I found it hard to find shirts that reached to my pants and still fit up top. Finding pants that would be long enough and snug enough around the waist was really hard. The way I dressed or wanted to dress was the area that my mom and I clashed the most. My mom is a teacher and is one of the most creative people I know. Being younger, I didn't see the shield she wanted to be for me. She wanted me to be portrayed for a godly young woman.

My high school made dress-code regulations and if you didn't go by them, you were sent to in-school suspension or sent home. I remember in my physical science class a boy constantly teasing me about how thin I was. One day he decided to tell the class that he knew what I wanted for Christmas and I could not have agreed more. He told everyone that I wanted a feeding tube that hooked to my backside and chest. Then he proceeded to tell the class that an air pump wouldn't hurt either. I desired to be desired. I wanted a figure that everyone loved and every girl wanted. I wanted to look in the mirror and be satisfied and it was many years before that actually happened.

My identity crisis occurred only a few months after I lost my first love. I began to see a guy in secret who I knew my parents wouldn't approve. He wasn't a Christian and our morals didn't reflect one another, but I excused those things simply because he offered undivided attention to me. He made me feel like the person I wanted to be and look like, even though I still didn't see that in the mirror. Six months before that relationship ended he revealed several things he was involved in, that went against everything I believed. Instead of fearing God and the consequences of sin, I began to cling to him more in high hopes I could change him. I suddenly changed from the center of his attention, to an invisible ghost.

Only His Light

How could I have not known that it was impossible to change anyone? I had been in church all my life. I should have known that God is the only one who can turn darkness into light. Lie after lie and hurt after hurt and trying every possible thing to hold onto to him that relationship ended, painfully. I felt like a failure because I hadn't changed him. I felt like I couldn't decipher what was the truth and what was a lie. Did he care for me? Did he think I was attractive? Did he really respect me for who I was and for who I wouldn't be? These thoughts and unanswered questions captivated my mind, day and night.

Depression was so thick and evident in my face, it was unbearable. I remember not even talking to classmates between classes just smiling a fake smile to keep people away. After crying out in desperation a little too loud, I found myself in therapy for about three months. The Lord placed a God-fearing woman to lead me to a peace that passes all understanding. She led me to a side that I had heard of but never experienced. That side was a place of calling and a plan that had been carefully crafted and planned out by the very powerful hand of God. I developed a deeper love and respect for my parents for allowing someone else to step into their daughter's life and help her in ways they couldn't.

I never allowed myself to see the darkness in my own life. I only saw it in everyone else's life. Throughout a painful and trying process of healing I willingly allowed God to expose the dark corners of my life and he revealed those places in love. Although I allowed God to heal the pain of this relationship I still hated who I was. I lost my drive to be more than average. I stopped dreaming about who I wanted to be and started to accept the lies that I could be nothing.

More

I was very involved in my youth group but wasn't getting all that I desired. I was past the struggle of peer pressure and past finding God. I had found God at a young age, now I wanted to feel like I had found myself as well. It was so frustrating to see my body as a maze. I could feel myself, see myself but I could not understand myself. I was lost in my own body.

I had so many people in my life telling me who I was and wasn't. Everyone seemed to have a piece to my puzzle, everyone, but me. My dream was to always be a doctor or nurse and that dream soon turned to a bitter thought. Every piece people kept trying to hand me formed that uncomfortable bulge. Little did I know that God had a calling that he would soon reveal to me. I was soon graduating and I had no idea what to do with my life. I remember one time on vacation with my mom, we looked all over the internet for schools with nursing degrees, and I had never felt such a strong pulling in my life. A pulling far, far away from searching, I didn't know how to tell my parents what I felt, so I kept quiet. My parents are very smart and organized people. Everything must be planned and organized. I didn't know how to tell them I couldn't do the one thing they always taught me to do, plan.

Just Me and…Me

My circle of closest girlfriends began to grow apart. I still had connections to a few of them but things were changing. Some were going off to college and others were going in directions that they didn't want me to be a part of. I was pained in every area of relationships.

My senior year I began to work with middle schoolers. I was under an awesome covering and began to learn things about ministry. I knew this was where God wanted me. I knew he was calling me to Inner City Ministry. I taught, preached, prayed, counseled and I just felt right and I felt secure.

There was a time where everyone and everything failed me. I began to see things in the church and around me that weren't right. I began to discover that almost all the people in my life I loved and treasured so much couldn't even tell me the truth. The people that were supposed to never hurt me or let me down were no where to be found. They had all left me. I was so hurt and abandoned; I could almost taste loneliness and pain. It was like I was carrying this contagious disease, a disease of pain that consumed everyone that was associated with me. This all happened when I discovered who I was in Christ. I realized at this time that it was o.k. to be who I was.

Just when I thought I was right where he wanted me, I felt almost uprooted. The hurtful words people spoke straight to my heart, replayed over and over for months. Things people said that were the opposite of what I had tried to be and do that I was not the friend I should have been, that my intensions were of evil and not of good, that I thought I knew more than I did, that I was jealous of others' happiness, that I was making decisions that would hinder my prosperity. My prayer changed very quickly for those whom I loved. I had to pray that God would bless those who cursed me and that I would love those who hated me. This was so hard. I prayed for mercy on those who testified falsely against me. I prayed for those who foolishly spoke lies behind my back. I had to pray for their prayers to be purified because I learned that Proverbs says that those who turn their ears from the law will have prayers of abomination. These people that wanted to be spoon fed sugar and cream were my burden. I could no longer be associated with a people who lacked vision because I was determined not to perish, (Proverbs 29:18).

Stoned

At this time in my life everyone was against me. The only way I can describe where I was in life is to describe where the woman in the Bible was, the woman who had been caught in the very act of sin. The whole town wanted to stone her yet; Jesus stepped in and asked the person without sin to cast the first stone. He then wrote in the sand. What did he write? I don't know but I do know what he wrote for me.

This is the best description I can think of. I was lying in the sand just like the woman in the Bible and when I looked up everyone around me was holding stones friends, family, church people, even myself. What was I guilty of? I was guilty of being me. Yes, I have been guilty of sin, but we are all guilty, yet I am pardoned. I am not talking about sin though. I was guilty of just being me. I was guilty of loving a man of God that Jesus had prepared for me to spend the rest of my life with. I was guilty for speaking the truth when others were speaking deceitful lies. I was guilty for worshipping God and leading young people to Him through freedom. I was guilty yet innocent at the same time.

I hope this makes sense! The stones everyone had in hand hurt more than any other time. I had to pay consequences for something. Why, because this time I was innocent. Has anyone ever hit you for something you did wrong? Probably and then after a while the sting goes away. But has anyone ever hit you for something you *didn't* do? Maybe, see with this kind of hit the sting goes away but the bruise can last forever.

The Curse vs. HIS Promise

These phrases and comments hurt. They brought me pain and I shed tears. I felt like a failure as a friend, an embarrassment to my family and a hopeless student. What I had to realize was that the things these people spoke over me were curses that did not have to become true. These people did not hold my future in the palm of their hand. My heavenly Father, Jesus Christ does. I now walk in my calling and my anointing confidently.

The Lord has promised me so much. My desire is that you and your children and your children's children will walk boldly in your promise, never fearing the curses and predictions humanity speaks.

On February 25, 2006, I was united with DeMario Hood of South Carolina. I met my groom at an altar before over 275 friends and family. I am happily married and we will walk together and fight through the obstacles of marriage and the hardships of life.

My name means; strong, able, mighty and like a pearl. A pearl can only be perfected at great price. I believe my name has a prophetic meaning. I have fought the hardships of friends and family objecting to my union in marriage because we represent two different races and two different cultures. I have been told that my children will be disadvantaged in life. I was cursed by a man who told me we would never make it in ministry, because 90 % of our ministry opportunities would be down the tube because we were an interracial couple. I could respond to each of these curses, but I refuse. I simply whisper the name Jesus, for demons tremble at that name. I rejoice for Satan is the root of these prejudices and curses and I know his evildoers must tremble and flee when they hear me speak His name over my future.

Castles in The Sand

While they were writing all of their *predictions* of my life, God was writing for me in the sand, His *promises* for my life. See it was Him who had prepared a man for me. It was Him who called me to ministry. It was my God who called me to help the hurting.

He wrote that I would be a mother to the motherless and that one day when I birth my own children that they would hold an anointing to deliver nations. He wrote that my burden for others will be used in powerful intercession. He wrote that the relationships that I allowed the enemy to destroy will be restored through his power. He wrote that I have so much to offer to the Body of Christ. He wrote that I am guilty yet through His blood I am mercifully pardoned. He wrote I am beautiful and no other woman could make my husband happier. He wrote I am ordained to minister to others by sharing the gospel of Jesus Christ. He wrote that if I continuously tithe he would bless me abundantly. He wrote that I do have what it takes to be in full-time ministry.

He wrote that those around me who hate me and persecute me, only need be loved through acts of kindness and prayer.

Right before my eyes my Savior, Jesus Christ, had built what looked like a beautiful castle. That castle represents the wealth of the wicked being stored up for the righteous. It represents all the millions of pieces to my puzzle, meshed together beautifully. You see, you can hold millions of grains of sand or you can take those grains and allow the creator of the universe to take the grains and craft your identity into a beautiful castle that you want to live in, all the time.

In other words you may have some pretty ugly situations or a horrific past or both, but He can take all of that and use it to craft together a beautiful future. Don't forget just behind the sandy shore there is always an ocean tide, but that tide comes and goes. Don't allow the tide to destroy what He is building for you. That tide only comes so far. The Bible tells us no weapon formed against us shall prosper. The tide can be your reminder or it can be a prosperous weapon. IT IS YOUR CHOICE!

I see people all the time who have spoken evil words to my face and to my back. I hear the rumors they spread about me. I know of the gossip they whisper. However, I hear it differently. I hear a roaring ocean tide that comes only so far and then rolls far away for I am marked with great price…His price.

P.S. God is so funny! Just for the record I work at a domestic violence shelter that has a twenty-four hour hotline and God has called me to the ministry. He always knows best. I always said I never wanted this for myself, but I couldn't feel more fulfilled. When I have to work the night shift and the phone rings awakening me to encourage someone I always say, "God, you are so funny!"

The Glass House

Eyes, eyes everywhere
Meet me with this awful stare
Look in so fast, and then look out
No one knows what I'm all about

Eyes, eyes everywhere
I'm blinded by their awful glare
I want to go but I don't know where
This life is awful, so unfair

Eyes, eyes all around
Around my body they surround
But no longer am I bound
For I was once lost, but now I'm found

Damaris Martinez was born in Secaucus, New Jersey but moved to Clearwater, Florida at just a month old. At the age of 14, her parents moved to Cleveland, TN where she now resides. She attends Lee University and is majoring in Business Administration. She has been involved in many things at Lee and hopes to get her Masters in Counseling after she graduates. Her family is very important to her and she enjoys laughing and spending time with them. She has one brother, Tony who is married to her sister-in-law, Carlie. Damaris has a heart for people and a passion to see them fulfill their destiny.

Chapter Five
Kidnapped

According to Webster's Dictionary, to kidnap means to seize and detain or carry away by unlawful force or fraud and often with a demand for ransom. In simple terms, that would be stealing something with no right to do so. Okay, so what do I mean by all these big terms? What I am trying to say is the enemy tried to kidnap my identity with absolutely no right to do so. In Jeremiah 1:5, the word of the Lord came to Jeremiah saying, "Before I formed you in the womb I knew you, before you were born I set you apart; I appointed you as a prophet to the nations." (NIV) The Bible says that "those who believed in His name, He gave the right to become children of God." (John 1:12 NIV) Although the enemy tried to convince me that I was nobody special, I stand according to the Word of God that says I am a child of God, set apart for His kingdom. Even though it wasn't that easy at first, this is my testimony.

Confused with Culture

People say that you find who you are in your family, your culture, and your background, but what if your family has a background of drugs, alcohol, and homosexuality. How is a person supposed to justify these things as being okay when the Bible says differently, while at the same time loving and accepting the family for the things that they do. Let me just tell you a little bit about myself. I am full-blooded Puerto Rican, both sides of my grandparents born and raised in Puerto Rico. I was born in New Jersey and raised in Florida, always knowing that I was different than most of the kids I grew up with. I wasn't black or white, and most people just figured that I just had a really nice tan. I never really knew who I could really relate to. As I began to get older, I realized that I was getting a lot of attention because of the way that I looked. People were telling me at such a young age that I had a unique look and should be a model. I remember my mom sitting me down when I was around six or seven years old, and telling me that it didn't matter how pretty I was on the outside, if I was unkind and mean on the inside that I would get ugly real fast. I always remembered those words but still was searching to fit in somewhere. In search for my identity, I began to do anything that I had to do in order to feel like I belonged somewhere, even if I had to lie to people.

Lost in Lies

Lying can overtake people; it becomes a defense mechanism that people begin to use unconsciously. It becomes a habit that is hard to break. The Bible says that the truth shall set you free (John 8:32). Somehow, someway the truth will always be revealed. So, what is the point of lying? Why do we as humans get so caught up in lies? Not just lies that we tell or people tell us, but lies from the enemy. I was not only caught up in lying to people, but I was caught up in believing the lies of the enemy. The lies I believed from the enemy are lies like, "I have to be pretty to accomplish anything in life," or "People have to think that I am awesome, before I can think I am awesome." These are merely just lies that fill our minds and cause us to live our lives trying to impress others and before we know it, we are living a lie. When I first entered high school, the temptation to get involved in sex, drugs, and alcohol was pretty heavy. Most of

64

it was indirect pressure that I felt, not necessarily direct peer pressure. Since I had just moved from Florida to Tennessee, I wanted to make new friends and fit right in. I noticed that there was not a lot of Puerto Ricans at my high school; everyone was either white or black. As I mentioned earlier, I really didn't have anyone to relate to, nowhere to necessarily fit right in. Eventually, I started to make friends and we were getting invited to parties every weekend. Upperclassmen were inviting us and junior and senior guys started to ask me out at these parties. I started to plot ways that I could get to parties or go to people's houses and do certain things without my parents finding out. Now, let me just inform you that I have two parents who are attorneys and very strong prayer warriors, so I don't know what I was thinking because, of course, they would catch me. Despite all these things, I still started to lie to my parents. You name it and I would make up a lie about it. I would say that I was going to my friend's house to spend the night, but instead we would be out till two in the morning trying to see every guy in town. I know that you know what I'm talking about, we all were doing it. Unlike my friends' parents who never did find out about the lies that their kids were telling them, somehow my parents knew exactly what I was trying to do. I believe it was by the grace of God. I would get caught time after time and get grounded time after time, but I still wasn't learning. I'd just think of a way that I could be sneakier next time. After many times of getting my car keys, cell phone, and computer taken away from me, I still wasn't learning my lesson. Sometimes I think that we have to learn things the hard way, and we don't know how something feels until somebody does it to us. Well, after all that lying I had been doing to my parents, I started to get lied to and it didn't feel too good.

Around my sophomore year of high school I started to date a guy that was a senior. He was very good looking, extremely popular, and an excellent athlete. Everybody knew him and talked about how pretty his eyes were and how good of a body he had. I was set with what I had always wanted and desired. The only problem was that he smoked, did drugs, drank, and was sexually active. I assured him that I was not going to get involved in any of those things and in order for us to be together he had to stop living the lifestyle he was living. I remember his exact words being, "If you just give me a chance, I will prove to you how I can change." Well, I will go ahead and let everyone reading this book know, that it is much easier for someone to bring you down than it is for you to pick them up and I never believed that. Once again, I was hard- headed and had to learn the hard way. We started dating and everything was going great, through my sophomore year and on to my junior year. My friends would always tell me how hot he was and how lucky I was to have gotten him. However, he continued to hang out with the same crowd. They were his boys that he had grown up with, and he would tell me that nothing would come between them. He would say that he could hang out with them and have no problem not smoking or drinking, even though that is what they were doing. Duh! How stupid could I possibly be! Let me tell you something, if you want to quit doing the things that you are doing that are not pleasing in the eyes of the Lord, you must separate yourselves from the people who are still doing it. I will get into that later on in the chapter. As I continued to believe that he had quit doing these things, I kept pursuing this relationship. He would try physical things with me and we ended up going farther than I wanted to go, but I still didn't lose my virginity which is a testimony in itself. He would tell me that if we were older, he would marry me and all sorts of things like that. Although I was very caught up in the world, my parents had instilled in me the Word of God and taught me how to always be in God's will. So, I began to pray about this relationship. I would say, "God, if it is not your will, then let me know somehow." Sometimes we ask God to reveal to us the right things to do, but we don't bother to listen to Him when He is trying to tell us. This is what I did; I simply was too caught up in this guy that I didn't notice all the things going on around me that would reveal the truth to me. About six months into the relationship, I started to feel this strong urgency to break up with him. People were asking me "Why? What did he do to you?" and I honestly couldn't give them an answer. I just knew in my heart that it was time. I broke up with him and it was a hard thing to do. A few weeks' later people started telling me that while we were together he was still doing drugs and still drinking. Come to find out, the entire six months that I and this perfect guy were together, he was lying to me. I had brought him to church with me and everything; he seemed to be doing fine while we were together. However, it was all a lie, he was living a lie and it didn't feel good once I found out about it. This is when I began to learn my lesson on lying. God's word never fails and it is true that the truth shall set you free. I came to my mom and my dad and apologized for all the times that I had lied to them and started to try my best to come to them with the truth. However, still in search for my identity, I still knew that I was getting attention someway or somehow and continued to feed off this attention. I like to say that I was "too hot to hear God."

Too Hot to Hear Him

I'm sure you can think of someone that you hang out with, who is always the center of attention. It doesn't matter what anybody else is doing, as long as people are paying attention to them. Everywhere you go they get all the attention and almost strive for it. The person I'm describing was exactly me. The problem was it got too far. I became "too hot." You might be thinking what in the world I'm talking about when I say "too hot," and some of you know exactly what I'm talking about. The hot I'm talking about is the hot I think when I'm on the beach and see a guy that looks good. You know, like when you're watching a music video and you see those guys or girls dancing and you're like, "Dang, he looks good," or "Wow, she is fine!" Okay, so where am I going with this? There was a time in my life when I was too hot to hear God, or at least I thought I was. As I mentioned earlier, I moved from Florida to Tennessee during the summer before high school. I was sad about leaving my friends, but excited about a new beginning. As I entered into high school, I discovered that I had a few curves and obviously something that was attracting guys to me. When I discovered these things, it went straight to my head. I tried to stay humble, but I was feeding off the attention I was getting from guys. My days began to consist of whose attention I could get this day, what guy I could get now, or how many guys I could talk to, without them finding out about each other. My friends started to make bets with me on who they thought I could or couldn't get. I became way too involved with guys, doing things that I shouldn't have been doing. Before I knew it, I was basing who I was upon how much attention I got. It was all about me, although I never would have admitted it.

This brings me to the story of Saul in the Bible. As I began to read and study the Word through a Bible study that I was going to, I learned about a man named Saul. In 1 Samuel 8, Israel asks for a King to rule over them. The Lord had already appointed Saul as King and told Samuel about him. When Samuel went to anoint Saul to become King over Israel, Saul asks why in chapter 9. He thought so little of himself and didn't understand why he was being chosen to become King over Israel. Saul had to have been a noble man for the Lord to appoint him as King over a nation. However, Saul didn't stay humble about it and in 1 Samuel 15; he sets up a monument in his own honor. When Samuel finds out about it he says in verse 17, "Although you were once small in your own eyes, did you not become the head of the tribes of Israel? The Lord anointed you king over Israel. ... Why did you not obey the Lord? Why did you pounce on the plunder and do evil in the eyes of the Lord?" Saul denies that he disobeys the Lord and begins to blame everything on everybody else. Samuel then replies in verse 23, "For rebellion is like the sin of divination, and arrogance like the evil of idolatry. Because you have rejected the Word of the Lord, he has rejected you as king." When I began to read and study this story, the Lord revealed to me that if I wasn't careful, this was starting to take place in my life. I was so caught up in the attention I got from people that my humility was starting to go away and it started to go to my head. Saul was doing things all wrong, but said he was doing things all right. Samuel rebuked him and told him "to obey is better than sacrifice." In verse 24, Saul admits that he didn't obey God because he was afraid of the people and gave in to them. I knew that I needed to start forgetting about myself and what others said about me and start focusing on what God wanted for my life. Saul found his identity in the fact that he was king over Israel and not in God. He found his identity in what he thought he had accomplished on his own without stepping back and realizing that it was the Lord who appointed him king in the first place. I started to realize that I never wanted to become like Saul. So caught up in myself and my own accomplishments that I forget to step back and look at who really got me where I am today.

Holding on to History

When I became sick and tired of being sick and tired, I took a step back and looked at my life; I knew that I was finding my identity in what other people said about me, not what God says about me. If you remember anything that I say in this chapter, remember to never let people and what they say eat away your identity. I had to constantly remind myself that I am not what other people say I am, I am who God says I am. I am not a product of what has happened to me or what others say about me. I am a product of God. His creation, from the time I was in my mother's womb. There are things that I started to fill my mind with, instead of the lies that the world was filling me with. I began to start to realize that I was fearfully and wonderfully made, no matter if I'm red, yellow, black, or white.

As I began to try and live by Romans 12:2, "Do not conform any longer to the pattern of this world, but be transformed by the renewing of your mind," it got a little hard. I still was hanging out with my same friends because they meant a lot to me. They had been through everything with me. I had heard all my life that bad company corrupts good character (1 Corinthians 15:33 NIV) and he who walks with the wise grows wise, but a companion of fools suffers harm (Proverbs 13:20 NIV). But it never really got into my spirit. I just figured that I would prove everyone wrong and I could still hang out with my old friends as long as I didn't get involved with the things that they were involved with. WRONG!!! I couldn't do it, I was still influenced by them and they weren't filling my mind with anything that was edifying for my spirit. I was still attached to my past while I was trying to move on in my destiny. What this is called is being lukewarm, neither hot nor cold. Revelation 3:16 says "So, because you are lukewarm—neither hot nor cold—I am about to spit you out of my mouth." (NIV) When I read this, not only did it scare me to death but I began to realize that I can't just do what I want to do, hang out with whomever I want to hang out with, and still be fit for the kingdom. I was falling in love with God, but still clung to my past. In Luke 9:61-62, a man decides to follow Jesus and asks Him if he can just go back to say good bye to his family. Jesus replied to that by saying, "Anyone who puts his hand to the plow and looks back is not fit for the kingdom of God." In 2 Peter 2:22, those who return to the world are compared to a dog returning to its vomit. I had to realize that yesterday has gone away and today is a new day. We can't get caught between who God calls us to be and who we used to be. We can't let our history hinder us from our destiny or else our destiny will never be fulfilled. Instead of wishing that everyone would like us, we need to start praying for the anointing. The purpose of the anointing is not to make man like us; it is to make the King like us.

There was a time when I felt like the Lord couldn't hear my cry, like he couldn't hear my prayers. The Bible says that he hears the prayers of the righteous. There was a time in the Old Testament where David feels like the Lord has forsaken him, he cries out in Psalm 22:1-2: "My God, why have you forsaken me?" Just like David, I felt alone. There were times that I thought there was nobody in sight. When all my old friends were hanging out, I had to come home because I knew that I was called to a higher standard. It was hard but it was times like this that made me who I am today. It was times like this that I took time to draw closer to God. The Bible says that the Lord will never leave you, nor forsake you (Hebrews 13:5-6); He is a friend that sticks closer than a brother (Proverbs 18:24). No matter how many people you feel have betrayed you, God promises that he will never turn his back on us. As long as we stay rooted in Him, He will guide our paths. (Proverbs 4: 25-27) "Let your eyes look straight ahead, fix your gaze directly before you. Make level paths for your feet and take only ways that are firm. Do not swerve to the right or to the left; keep your foot from evil."

A Divine Destiny

The devil will do his utmost to keep your destiny from being fulfilled. When you know who you are in Christ and start to walk in His will, it may get hard, it will become a constant battle, but it will also become a constant victory. Let me tell you a story of how the devil tried his utmost to destroy my destiny. One of my closest friends and I were coming back from a vacation in Florida. While she was asleep in the back seat I was just listening to some Kirk Franklin while I was driving. I began to get this urgency to pray and so I just started to pray a hedge of protection over the car and that no weapon formed against us would prosper. My friend all of a sudden woke up and I asked her why she woke up. She replied that for some reason she just couldn't fall asleep. Not two minutes later, a car began to come right into my lane. I was apparently in her blind spot and she had no idea that she was coming right into my car. We were right in the middle of Atlanta traffic which was flowing pretty heavily. When she started to come in to my lane I yelled "What should I do?!?" I panicked and swerved the steering wheel to the left not thinking that it would make our car swerve into the next lane. There were cars all around me and I don't understand exactly how things happened after that moment, but I know that we ended up spinning around twice across two lanes of traffic on the interstate. We ended up facing the opposite direction of traffic and we were not touched. We were completely safe not even harmed by another car. Immediately a police car pulled to the side of the road that had seen the entire thing and didn't understand how we did not get hit. My friend had not had on her seat belt the entire time and she was completely safe, not hurt at all. What I am trying to say to you is that the enemy tried to hurt us and keep our destiny from being fulfilled, but I am a living testimony that God has a bigger plan! Now that I am starting to walk in His will, the enemy is mad. Stuff like this did not happen when I had no clue who I was, when I was searching for my identity in what people said about me and not what God said about me. That is no coincidence. Whoever is reading this book needs to know that your destiny is much greater than the world tells you it is. You are called to live in a higher standard than the world. Our generation is a chosen generation that has been called to come out of the world and be separate from the rest. Stand out and be humble, love others as we love ourselves.

Thanks to God the enemy cannot have my identity. As I mentioned in the beginning of the chapter, to kidnap means to seize and detain or carry away by unlawful force or fraud and often in demand for ransom. However, we are so blessed to know that Jesus paid the ransom for us over 2,000 years ago when He died on the cross. The enemy doesn't have to have our identity. Even though I felt kidnapped, like I couldn't get out of the temptation I was constantly facing, the Lord reached down and picked me up. And for that, I am so thankful! Now I have a passion to travel the world and speak the gospel to nations. I can see myself feeding those who are hungry and clothing those who are cold and have nothing to keep them warm. Now all I am doing is being a vessel for God, to win souls to the kingdom.

Brandon M. Perritte is attending Lee University and pursuing a Christians Ministry degree with a Pastoral emphasis. Brandon's goal is to one day plant and pastor a church in an urban city. He understands and realizes that the process to obtain his goal will take time and is now working towards his degree. He is striving to be in God's will and to study to show himself approved.

Chapter Six
What If...

What if while you were reading this chapter you began to feel life breathed back into you, filling your life with hope? What if strongholds were released in your life that you've been wrestling with for years? What if every negative word spoken over your life began to leave your mind and peace filled your thoughts? What if a healing happened that you've been expecting for a long, painful time? What if your marriage is mended, your son or daughter comes off drugs, or your family is restored? What if you find out who you are, not who your parents or family members want you to be but who you are in God and what He wants you to become in Him?

What I have come to understand is that your identity is up to you and your choices. The Bible says in Psalms 139:14,"We are all fearfully and wonderfully made." Not one of us is alike. Through this journey called life, you find out who you are and who God wants you to be through the choices you make. The choice is yours. My question is while you read this chapter, what is, your what if?

The Fight Begins

Jeremiah 1:5 states, "Before you were in your mother's womb, I knew you. Before you were born I set you apart. I anointed you as a prophet to the nations." I quoted this Scripture to say God has a reason for everything, great or small. Reasons only God can explain as to why we go through what we do. Everyone has a testimony to share, their personal story. Without a test you have no *testimony*. In this chapter, all I am sharing with you is my testimony of what I have gone through and how I won every battle because of God. If God be for me, who can be against me?

Before you begin to read I would like to pray a prayer over you. *"Father, I thank You for each individual reading this book. I ask You as they read that You begin to reveal Yourself to them in such a mighty way. Reveal to them from Revelation that we are over comers by the blood of the Lamb and the word of our testimony. Through You, we are more than conquerors by Your strength. I thank You in advance for what You are going to do in our lives. It's not a coincidence they are reading this book. You have divinely set them up to encourage them, equip them, and inspire them to fight the good fight of faith. Give them peace where there is no peace; give them joy where there is no joy. I pray this in Your mighty Name, amen."*

Get comfortable with it and move on

My goal for you is to learn that transparency is the best key to overcoming any battle you are facing. You have to learn to be comfortable with your history to overcome it. The only way to become comfortable with your history is to be real and face it. The past is the past and that can't be changed. It doesn't matter if the private pain was self inflicted or caused by someone else.

I am reminded of the story in Exodus 4 of when God and Moses were alone in the desert. God asked Moses what he had in his hand. Moses responds with, a rod. The culture in those days was for the shepherd's rod to record the shepherd's history, His life's triumphs and defeats. His history was recorded somewhat like this. Moses was a slave born as a Hebrew brought up as an Egyptian. Once he was rich and experienced being poor, a murderer at the age 40. God asks Moses to throw his rod, his history down. So Moses threw his rod down. When he did, it turned into a snake and Moses got scared. God said, now pick it up. So Moses fearfully picked up his fear, the snake and it turned back into a rod. Repeatedly God asked Moses to pick up the rod and each time he did it turned into his fear. What God was trying to prepare Moses for was he would one day have to face his history and become comfortable with who he was. You can't move to the next level in God until you become comfortable with where you've come from. God was preparing Moses to stand before his fear, Pharaoh, to walk in faith not in fear. Moses faces Pharaoh timidly, on behalf of his people he states, let my people go. He threw down his rod and it turned into a snake. Pharaoh said, I have a rod also and throws his rod down, too. It, too, turns into a snake. Moses' snake eats Pharaoh's snake. The moral of the story is when you face your history even in fear, your adversary the devil tries to scare you and fight you, but God will consume him on your behalf. The battle belongs to the Lord. Don't fear your history! Overcome it!

I haven't gone through what I've gone through to keep it to myself. Neither have you. God wants to encourage you as He has me in whatever you've gone through or going through, He is with you!

What I have gone through has made me who I am today in Christ. I am stronger today because of Him. I am at peace today because of Him. I am victorious today because of Him. And so can you. If the enemy of my soul couldn't kill me while I was in the world, he definitely isn't going to be able to kill me now. He should have gotten me when I was down. I'm still standing!

My journey

I grew up in a Christian home with a heritage of generational preachers and missionaries. You wouldn't think it would be hard for me to lose my identity in the world with such a surrounding. Let me tell you, your family members can't save you. They can pray you through whatever it is you will be going through or are currently going through but they can't save you. There is only one Savior and His name is Jesus Christ. Life is all about choices and God has given you the ability to make wise choices if you will just listen and learn from His ways and wisdom from His Word. The choices you make are up to you and the power of the will.

Choose LIFE

If I could paint my life on a blank canvas, I would have painted it differently. You just don't plan on bad things happening to you. At least if you are optimistic like me. Before I was born my fate was in the hands of one woman, my mother, outside the Sovereignty of God. At the young age of 19, she decided to have sex and she wasn't married. When reading her chapter you understand she made the appointment to abort me. Thank God she chose life.

The devil tried to steal her seed. I am that seed. The enemy knew the destiny on my life and that souls would be added to the kingdom through this testimony so he tried to abort my life. God won and I was born on December 14, 1983. Life was breathed into these lungs and started me on my journey that has been hard but has been worth it all, even to the end, eternity.

The curse stops here

When I was born, I was diagnosed with an eye disorder. A disease called ocular albinism. What in the world is that, you ask. Basically in layman terms, I'm legally blind. This particular disease is from an STD (sexually transmitted disease). You can trace this curse from years ago to the current generation. It truly is a generational curse. The sins of a father passed down. One of my past relatives chose to have an affair with another woman, brought it home to his wife. When she conceived and gave birth, she didn't know that she was a carrier of the disease because her husband tried to hide his sin. Be sure your sins will find you out! Unfortunately, the selfishness not only affected him but the generations to come. The genetic research reveals that women are the carriers and it is linked to be found in the first born boy. I relate it to being like a terrorist attack. It's an enemy placed where it shouldn't and it's my responsibility to expose it, pray it out and break the curse for the rest of the generations to come.

What time is it?

All of my life I have dealt with this attack. For the longest time it was just a distraction to detour me from my destiny. I hated being in special services at school. I didn't want to be special. I promise you, if I've been through one healing line I've been through twenty or more. I've gone to healing crusades. Closed my eyes and begged God to heal me. Only to leave disappointed with the same eyesight.

I had to face my history. Unless God chooses to heal me and I know He will because His timing is perfect, I walk in His peace and provision that He is in control, not me. I am not complaining but trying to encourage someone who has or is walking through something just like me who believes but in the natural has yet to see the manifestation of His promise. I have a special message from what I believe the Lord would encourage you with today, "Keep on holding on because the battle is not yours God says it's mine. When the time is right I will perform my promise. I will do it. Don't doubt but keep walking in faith for when you can handle it, I will give it to you."

I felt the Lord speak to my spirit and tell me in 2004 when He heals my eyes it will break the curse. He persisted to say, I am the key to the healing door. Let me tell you, no matter what your situation is great or small, I serve a God who can do anything. He is the God of all flesh, and nothing is too hard for Him, Jeremiah 32:27. The timing of God is everything, Ecclesiastes 3:3, "To everything there is a season."

Hebrews 11:1 says, "Now faith is the substance of things hoped for the evidence of things not yet seen." The devil will try to convince you, that you don't have enough faith. The devil is the father of lies. Keep believing and pressing into God, and praying for it. It's on the way. It only takes the size of a mustard seed to move a mountain. Imagine what little faith it would take to kill cancer, restore your marriage, pray your children off drugs. Let me ask you, what is your, what if? What if God doesn't heal me, what if, God doesn't restore my marriage, what if, God doesn't bring my children back home, you may ask? Keep on believing!

The choice to split

Not only was I dealing with being a special child with special needs, but my parents decided when I was two to divorce. My mother and I left North Dakota where I was born and moved to Cleveland, Tennessee to start all over, a new life. Little did I know this is where I would find out who I really was in this journey called life.

Being single is tough when going through a divorce much less having to raise a child alone. Mom and I were really close. Everywhere she went she took me. I remember one day when she had to go to work her dropping me off at the daycare. I pulled so hard on her clothes I about pulled her skirt off. She said she cried more than I did that day. It was just as tough for her, too.

As I reflect back on my childhood I remember going to elementary school. Nobody was really different in my eyes. Whether my friends were black, white, rich or poor, split home or normal home, whatever that was, really didn't matter to me. My norm was my father would come up every other weekend and take me back to Atlanta where he and his new wife were living at the time. My mom remarried too. I don't have horror stories of my parents hating each other and step parents beating me. What I do remember is they tried to make this unfortunate situation as pleasant as they could. There is no doubt in my mind the decision they made to split and be divorced was the best for them. I have a great step mom and a great step dad. My parents found someone else who was obviously a better mate for them who God designed them to be with.

What's my name?

I was six years old when my mom remarried. My friends and family in Atlanta knew me as Brandon Perritte. My friends in Cleveland where I lived with my mom knew me as Brandon Kramer. As a young boy this can be very confusing. Where do I fit in? Where do I belong in this huge picture? I felt so torn. I never wanted to hurt any of my parents therefore; I just tried to make everyone happy. I would just change my name wherever I went. Some places I was a Perritte and other places I was a Kramer.

When I started middle school which is such a hard age anyway, I felt like my whole life began to change. I was popular in elementary school. I had grown up with all my friends ever since kindergarten. When I enrolled in middle school we were all split up and it seemed like I was the only one that was left out of the group. I felt like I was in another country. I made new friends which isn't a big deal for me since I love to be with people. Unfortunately, I made the wrong ones. Cool kids were hard to come by and since I thought I was so cool I wanted to find cool friends to relate to. My old friends accepted my eye disorder. They would often times even help me out when I couldn't see something. My right eye is what doctor's call a lazy eye. When I get real tired people can tell by my right eye. Always wanting to fit in and be accepted by everyone, it seemed to be getting harder. I remember one night crying to my mom before I went to sleep because cruel kids at school would make fun of me. It was a devastating time. I felt weird, like the elephant man, isolated and distorted, definitely not normal. One day in the cafeteria at school I remember a fellow class mate snapping his fingers at me and in front of everyone asking me, "Hey, Brandon, are you looking at me. I'm over here, no over here." The mocking was unbearable. I begged my mom to take me out of public school and put me into a private school where I was accepted. My church friends accepted my disability. What I understood was just because the building is labeled a Christian school not all kids are Christ like. This is where the beginning of my curious mind became my worst enemy.

I convinced my mom to enroll me into the Christian private school. I tried out for the basketball team and made it. I became the star of the basketball team. That sounds really good huh? The school only had about 25 students. Being the ladies man that I was, one of the cheerleaders started liking me and it seemed like everything was going great until reality set in and I was failing my classes. Being the star basketball player was a short lived dream, but it sure felt good while it lasted.

So back to public schools I go the second semester of my freshman year. I felt like a stranger in my own country once again. All of my old friends had grown up together while I was still finding my place to fit in. I wanted to play basketball in the public schools. The school was segregated in its own way; if you weren't black or over 6ft. 3 you didn't play. I wasn't tall enough nor was I black. I just wanted to run, run as far as I could and never stop, somewhat like Forrest Gump in the movie. So I chose to swim. I was really good at swimming. Swimming for the city team when I was younger prepared me to swim with the school team.

The feeling of rejection

A year or so had gone by and I made new friends. Friends and people in general were very important to me. The feeling of people leaving you when you are young was very scary to me. What I am about to share, is to not bring shame or blame on either sides of my parents but to let you understand the pain a child experiences when going through a split, a divorce. I felt empty inside. A void seemed to always be in my life. I knew I was loved. I was just trying to work through so many emotional issues at such a vulnerable time in my life of growing up. All I wanted to find was someone to fill this void. I found a group of guys that when I met them we just clicked. We were the fearsome five. Still trying to find my place in life and where in this world did I fit in, I found myself doing some really stupid things. While attending the Christian school I started smoking cigarettes once in a while at the age of 14. My mom found out and I got into trouble but I really didn't care. I was going to do what I wanted to do. It didn't stop there. I was always told that cigarettes would never be enough and sure enough it wasn't. My new found friends smoked and that didn't help my surrounding or my cravings. How I swam and smoked at the same time, only God knows how, but I did it and broke school records.

My life became consumed with my new friends. We did everything together. I was one of the oldest so I felt like a leader. I was not a very good one but being a part of this group made me feel needed. My void seemed to subside a bit. By my senior year I was still smoking, drinking and now doing drugs. I lost my virginity and really didn't care what happened to me. Before I knew it I was over my head with trouble and really didn't care if I got out of it. It was like the snowball affect. My curiosity started out small then it kept getting bigger, and bigger and bigger. The more I tried the bigger my desire to try more stuff increased, until it seemed to become so big I couldn't stop and the snowball was huge. I didn't have the strength to stop it so I rolled with it.

For the next two years I began to continue to experiment with everything that the world had to offer. I wanted to totally be sold out to the world. My goal as a hellion was to try to do every drug there was. I turned down a swimming scholarship at Georgia Southern University (GSU) because I was so caught up in my selfishness. My plot to fill this void seemed to be by my own destruction. I stopped going to church whenever I could get away with it. And when I did go, my mom would make me sit on the front row with the family. Running with the devil during the week and sitting on the front row on Sundays. Who in the world am I?

I don't tell you any of this to brag or give praise to the enemy for what I did. I know there is someone out there who played church like me doing the same stuff I did. I want to tell you whoever you are, you don't have to go through the torment and drugged up sleepless nights anymore. The world doesn't show the picture of when you go home from the party and you have mixed so many drugs together that you aren't sure you'll wake up. The world doesn't show you the haunting spirits around you as you lie in your bed at night scared, petrified they would consume you. If you feel a void in your life the only one who can fill that void is Jesus Christ. He knows what you are going through. He really does feel your pain. Look to Him for your strength. If He thought you could make it on your own, He wouldn't have had to die on a rugged cross. He did it so you could be free from yourself.

The root of rejection is a horrible pain. Today I still have to deal with private pain in parts of my life that pertain to rejection. Releasing the pain to Jesus is a daily process. Miracles happen instantly, healing is a process. I know I am safe with Him.

I have many stories, testimonies, in my life I could have shared with you of how God brought me through. I felt Holy Spirit wanting to encourage someone who has gone through a personal handicap, a divorce, the feeling of rejection and a void that needs to be filled with Jesus.

My goal now is to be totally sold out to Christ. I want to be able to use my history to destroy any devil that tries to detour me from my destiny. When he tries to remind me of my past I remind him of his future.

What if you chose to believe God instead of the lies of the enemy? What if you chose to surrender instead of fight with the will of God in your life? What if you chose to face your history and release your fears to Jesus? What if you chose to forgive those who have hurt you? What if Jesus Christ came back today, where would you spend eternity? Find your identity in Him.

What if....I hadn't been born?

Chapter Seven
The Lost Coin – The Lost You

Do you know how valuable you are? Jesus talked in parables so we could understand clearly what He was trying to express to us. What is a parable? A parable is a brief allegory to teach a moral lesson. What is an allegory? An allegory is an extended metaphor, especially a story in which a fictional character and actions are used to understand and express aspects of concepts relating to human existence. Parables often times begin with; it is like unto...Jesus used the word *like* even before it was *like* cool. Who says He can't relate to the valley girl or surfer dude.

Jesus speaks to us from the book of Luke 15:8-9, "Or what woman, having ten (silver) drachmas, (each one equal to a day's wages), if she loses one coin, does not light a lamp and sweep the house and look carefully and diligently until she finds it? And when she has found it, she summons her (women) friends and neighbors, saying, rejoice with me, for I have found the silver coin which I had lost."

It is very easy as we grow older to lose ourselves, our identity in others. Our childhood forms us and we act out what we have learned in our adolescent years. These years of our lives are so impressionable. We are formed and shaped by what people say we are or what we will become. I am reminded of a joke sent to me via email from a close friend of mine called, "The Southern Grandma."

In a trial, a Southern small-town prosecuting attorney called his first witness, a grandmotherly, elderly woman to the stand. He approached his witness, and asked her, "Mrs. Jones, do you know me?" She responded, "Why, yes, I do know you Mr. Williams. I have known you since you were a young boy, and frankly, you have been a big disappointment to me. You lie, you cheat on your wife, and you manipulate people and talk about them behind their backs. You think you are a big shot when you haven't the brains to realize you will never amount to anything more than a two-bit paper pusher. Yes, I know you." The lawyer was stunned! Not knowing what else to do, he pointed across the room and asked, "Mrs. Jones, do you know the defense attorney?" She again replied, "Why, yes, I have known Mr. Bradley since he was a youngster, too. He's lazy, a bigot, and he has a drinking problem. He can't build a normal relationship with anyone and his law practice is one of the worst ones in the entire state. Not to mention he cheated on his wife and three different women. One of them was your wife. Yes, I know him." The defense attorney almost died. The judge asked both counselors to approach the bench and, in a very quiet voice, said, "If either of you idiots asks her if she knows me, I'll send you to the electric chair."

Perhaps these men didn't have a great role model in their lives to teach them morals and ethics.

At the age of 16, a minister prophesied over my life at a camp meeting. For those of you who have not grown up within a church environment, a camp meeting is where church members gather all over the state during the summer for one week or so to have church. The word was I would minister to the multitudes. When I wasn't walking in my destiny, my mother would question the words spoken over my life. But she always held on to those words even when she saw me walking down the road of my very own personal detour.

I remember when I was growing up my mother would cook breakfast for us, sausage with eggs mixed in and grits. Now if you are not from the South you might not understand what grits are. My sister and I would come down before getting ready for school, eat breakfast and have devotions with my mom. I am very thankful for those impressionable years when she poured the Word into us. It was the Word spoken over me when I was younger that returned me back to my destiny. To this day I rehearse the Scriptures instilled in me.

I knew I was valuable to my parents as I was growing up. I was always surrounded by acceptance and unconditional love. But somehow I lost myself in the midst of my journey. As I reflect back, it all stemmed from my low self-esteem because of my weight. I thought I was not valuable if I was fat. Who is going to love me? I don't measure up to perfection. My low self-esteem carried over into my dating life then on into my marriage. I found myself being possessive and very angry. I was angry at myself for being so foolish. I didn't know I had a temper until I got married. It was no ones fault but my own. I had a stronger will than the Word instilled in me to pursue my own adventures, my own demise. It wasn't because of my parents doing something right or wrong. I was my own enemy. I am the personality type where it is better to repent and say you are sorry rather than to ask permission. I had to repent plenty of times. Thank God for His amazing grace.

Circumstances in life sometimes cause you to lose something. For me it was myself. I had lost me. I hadn't really found me because I didn't take the time to know me. What have you lost? The woman who lost her coin, a day's wages, was frantically searching for what she had lost. We lose ourselves in our children, our husbands, our occupations, peer pressure, society's impressions until we believe that is what we are. That is not true. That is what we do. We are mommies, wives, employees, best friends, and lovers to our husbands or wives. In actuality we are God's creation made in His likeness. I didn't like myself much less think God would like me either. I always say, "I don't just love my husband, I like him too." Those you like you love to be with. Do you like you? Liking yourself means you like yourself enough to take care of yourself for you. Lose weight for you, exercise for you, read the Word for you, go shopping (without going in debt) for you and don't feel guilty about it. You are your best investment. What you do today prepares you for your future. If you are not taking care of yourself today, you will pay for it tomorrow. In my adolescent years I did things to my body to be thin, as you read in the first chapter. Today, I am paying for my foolishness. I speak from personal experience as a witness to attest to what will come to you if you don't take time to take care of yourself. When we are young, we think we are invincible or have you ever thought that would never happen to me. Sexually transmitted diseases are real, aids is real, and addictions are real. Don't play Russian roulette with your life. You are way too valuable for that. The word value means, to be of great worth. Do you think Jesus Christ had nothing else to do the day He was beaten beyond recognition for you or the 39 stripes that were carved in His back because you weren't valuable or of great worth? Do you know of anyone else that would do that for you?

If you have lost yourself, it is time to find yourself. It doesn't matter how old you are. Don't wait until you are in your twenties like I was before you know who you are and what God says about you. That one sentence will save you so much heartache. Take heed and listen to wisdom. Be wise and search for yourself like the woman in Luke 15. You are worth more than a lost coin. You are worth more than a day's wages. You are valuable.

I had one mother come up to me and say to me regarding her daughter, look at my daughter how beautiful she is, and truly she was, but she doesn't think so as she dropped her head. How can I help her to see her inward beauty? This young girl has a heart after God, she loves Him, dances with Him and for Him and yet she still doesn't feel pretty. My response was we have to get the knowledge from her head to her heart. There are a lot of young daughters of God who have head knowledge of Him but not heart knowledge of God. I told that young girl the only way you can get your head knowledge to your heart is a simple answer. It's not complex but it takes effort. You simply have to spend time with God. That's all. With all the effort and diligence it would take to find the lost coin use that same energy to diligently find Him. Give Him your time. Let's bring this to a point of relativity. When you find a young guy/girl you like what do you do? You talk on the phone, you spend every waking moment with that person, and you can't wait until they call you or see you again. Why? It's because you have fallen in love with them. Fall in love with your heavenly Father. You can't help but fall in love with Him when you spend time with Him. He is amazing. He is crazy about you. He can't wait until you wake up and say His name in the morning. He is a jealous God and He has to share you with so many things and people. Spending time with your heavenly Father is where you will find your value. Christ paid a price for you at a place called Calvary. Your destiny as a sinner was sold to slavery as a prisoner of your own selfishness but Christ paid the price for you. If you are having a hard time finding you, search for Christ. When you search for Christ you will find yourself in Him.

You have a choice to make. You don't have to be lost anymore. The moral of the parable of the Lost Coin is if one rejoices over a lost coin, how much more will your heavenly Father rejoice over you when you find Him. He isn't playing games like hide and seek from you nor does He have a hammer or gavel in the heavens waiting to hit you over the head with every time you make a mistake. Your heavenly Father's arms are intimately open wide for you to run to Him, jump in His arms and hug Him so tightly and never let go. He is waiting for you. You are more valuable than silver or gold.

This parable reminds me of one morning I was praying and I remembered the wall you see at Wal-Mart that says if you have seen this person call 1-800-THE-LOST. Unfortunately, the wall is filled with people's faces of all ages, race and gender with their names, height, weight and description the type of clothes they were last seen in. I felt sad in my heart and spirit about those that were lost. Suddenly, I was brought to tears when in the way I hear my Savior speak to me I heard Him say, "Baby girl, (because that is what He calls me sometimes), that is the way my heart hurts. I miss my children that are lost." It was like a vision that unfolded to me when He said come with me and let me show you something. Of course, I followed Him and he walked me into this beautiful room and there was a huge wall. It was like the living room of heaven unfolded right before my eyes. On the left hand side it had pictures of people from all races, gender, names and faces. I could see His hand print on the picture where smears of tears covered the outside of the picture like a parents who had love for their child they hadn't seen or heard from in a long time. He said, "These are the children for whom I intercede. I miss them." I could see tears streaming down His face while He longed for His children that He loves so much. He continued to say, some have walked with me before and they can't find me because of their own weakness of humanity. They won't seek me anymore and they have given up. I desire so desperately to place their picture on this wall. The wall my Savior turned to was to His right. I saw sons and daughters who have made their way back home. To my surprise I saw my picture there. He said, "Sandi, you were on the wall on the left until that day you surrendered to me and accepted me back into your life. I called the angels over and showed them your picture as I was taking it from the left wall to the right and we all celebrated you as the heavens thunderously rejoiced that glorious day. Thank you, Sandi, for never giving up on me, because I never gave up on you." Of course, in my quite time with my Savior I was weeping over what He so graciously showed me.

Isn't it time your Savior, Jesus Christ moves your picture from the left hand side of the wall to the right hand side of the wall so heaven can rejoice over you? Once you were lost, isn't it time to be found? Choose Christ. I want to see you there.

Perhaps you have found yourself in the chapters of this book in the triumphant stories and lives of these precious individuals. Maybe you are a people pleaser, wanting at all cost to make someone happy or possibly you are waiting for your God-man and not settling for the Good-man. Possibly you are from a divorced home or an orphanage raised by someone else besides your natural parents. Or maybe you are puzzled or misunderstood or confused by someone's theology of how life is truly supposed to be? Whatever your situation consists of, God is bigger than any problem, chaos or circumstance. Dysfunctional families are not a new revelation to God. From the garden when sin entered into the heart of Eve and she acted out her fleshly desires, is when dysfunction entered into the picture frame of families. Whatever hindrances, interferences or ailments keeping you from fulfilling your divine purpose know this from the prophet Jeremiah 32:27 – "Behold, I am the God of all flesh; nothing is too hard for me." Trust Him and you will find Him faithful.

May the God of peace fill your heart and mind as you passionately pursue Him and His purpose for your life and may the revelation of who He is enlighten you to a greater understanding of His love for you. Be blessed.